GETTING WET

Getting Wet

TALES OF LESBIAN SEDUCTIONS

anthologized by

Carol Allain
and Rosamund Elwin

women's
PRESS

CANADIAN CATALOGUING IN PUBLICATION DATA
Getting wet
ISBN 0-88961-170X
1. Lesbians' writings, Canadian (English). * 2. Short stories, Canadain
(English) – Women authors. 3. Short stories, Canadian (English).*
4. Canadian fiction (English) – 20th century.* 5. Lesbianism – Fiction.
I. Allain, Carol, 1962 – . II. Elwin, Rosamund, 1955 – .

PS8323.L47G48   1992   C813'.0108353   C92–094129–X
PR9197.35.L47G48   1992

Idyll: Four Days, by Chrystos reprinted with permission from *Dream On*
published by Press Gang Publishers.

Coyote Learns A New Trick, by Beth Brant reprinted with permission
from *Mohawk Trail* published by Firebrand Books and Women's Press.

Latex and Lube, by Karen X. Tulchinsky was previously published in
Angles Lesbian Literary Supplement.

Poem for Pat/on seeing an o'jays concert in buffalo by Karen Augustine
was previously published in *Fireweed*.

Lesbian Love Monologue by Muriel Miguel is excerpted from the stage
play *Hot'n'Soft*.

Copyright © 1992 Women's Press
Editor: Mona Oikawa
Copy editor: Tamai Kobayashi
Cover design: Grace Channer (with the assistance of Sunday Harrison)
Cover art: Grace Channer

This book was produced by the collective effort of Women's Press.
Women's Press gratefully acknowledges the financial support of the
Canada Council, the Ontario Arts Council and the Lesbian and Gay
Community Appeal.

Printed and bound in Canada
8 9 0 IML 01 00 99 98 97

CONTENTS

INTRODUCTION

This is a collection about sex. Lesbian sex. It's an adventure into the sexual imagination of lesbians, a journey created out of the desire to make public lesbian eroticism and sexuality. These are tales of seductions, woman to woman, set in locations where lesbians seek out and seduce each other. In bars and airports, subways and libraries, laundromats and on the job — even in bedrooms. The power of lesbian sexuality challenges the senses and envelops the body in pleasurable experiences that are written in a language that seduces the reader and leaves her wanting to read more.

The process of generating sexual literature for lesbians is one that is both fully underway and at the beginning of what we hope will be a long and an expansive mapping of desire. One Canadian anthology of lesbian erotica in English has been published to date; as of this writing, material is being solicited for another. *Getting Wet* takes its place in the expanding network of lesbian sex fiction as a book that embodies commitments to bringing lesbian lives together, representing race and class, and exploring the myriad of ways in which lesbians imagine sexuality.

As editors we worked from a strong commitment to producing a collection that is accessible to a wide range of readers. We were also motivated by our desire to make a space for lesbians where we can imagine — sexually. Although lesbian sexuality is now being inscribed in literature at an exponential rate — compared to the previous five hundred years — there is still a dearth of fiction about lesbian sexuality. *Getting Wet* expands the positive imagining of lesbians as sexual beings, healthy and aggressive, forthright and funny.

As this anthology shows, not all lesbians live in cities where there are dyke bars and women's dances. We hope this collection will reach lesbians who are living in rural areas, we hope it will help to bridge the spaces between lesbians, linking lesbian imaginations across gaps of all kinds.

Carol Allain
Rosamund Elwin

Latex and Lube

KAREN X. TULCHINSKY

I am in San Francisco on a long awaited vacation. I am staying with my friends, B.J. and Janice, in their two-bedroom flat over a liquor store in the Haight-Ashbury district. It is my second night in town and I am rested and ready for anything. I have told all my friends back home in Vancouver that I am going to pick up a San Franciscan woman, a complete stranger, and take her home for a night of hot, wild, anonymous, California sex. I decide that tonight is the night. My friends are in the next room, watching *China Beach* on TV, while I get ready for a night on the town.

I already know what I will wear. I am naked, drying myself off from a shower. I put down the towel and slip into a pair of very tight, faded, and ripped blue 501 jeans. I search the pockets of my suitcase for my one pair of black socks, put them on, and then squeeze into a pair of freshly shined cowboy boots. I find my tightest white t-shirt and pull it over my head, smoothing the bottom into the waist of my jeans. My black leather chaps fit snugly over my pants. A little gel in my hair and I'm almost ready. On the bed sits my toy bag, enticing me to take some of its contents out tonight.

I unzip the leather bag and remove a small leather pouch. It is designed to be worn on a belt and has a number of small compartments with special places for half a dozen latex gloves, three mini tubes of *Probe*, and several condoms or dental dams. I smile at myself in the mirror, a modern dyke, prepared for anything. I go over to a dresser on the other side of the room where I pop a tape into a cassette player. Out of the speakers, I can hear the opening chords of a popular song by Prince. I decide to try a practise run with my safe sex equipment. I do not want to find myself in the arms of a gorgeous babe, struggling to fit a glove on my hand.

There is an art, I decide, to practising erotic safe sex. I pick up a glove, and while Prince is singing "Women and girls rule my world, yes they rule my world," I stand, facing the bedroom mirror, snapping latex gloves onto my right hand with my left, one after the other, until I feel like a master. Then the *piece de resistance*: from inside my bag, I withdraw a medium-sized, soft rubber dildo fastened to a custom-made harness that fits around my hips, bikini style, allowing me to penetrate a woman while keeping my hands free for other things. Before concealing it in a secret pocket on the inside of my leather jacket, I try rolling a condom down its length a few times, until I feel confident that, in the heat of a passionate moment, I will be able to repeat the action with skill and grace.

I finish getting dressed and then go into the other room to model for Janice and B.J. They ooh and aaah appropriately and tease me a little before sending me off into the night. It is just a short walk to the Castro and the night is still young. I take my time, browsing in the card shops along the gay men's strip. I go into a men's sex toy shop and look around at the cards and calendars. Various wrist bands and other leather accessories are displayed in a glass case by the cash. I ask the fag behind the counter to show me a cock ring.

"I don't mean to be rude honey," he says to me, "but what does a dyke need with a cock ring?"

"It fits on my wrist … see?" I snap it on my left arm. "And they're cheaper than most wrist bands."

"Well, how do you like that?" he says, shaking his head and smiling.

"I'm an out of town dyke on the prowl tonight. Looking for women. Where do you think I should go?" I ask him.

"Amelia's, I guess," he answers.

My friends had suggested the same club, so it's off to Amelia's I go.

When I get there, I am sweating from the walk. I unzip my jacket and stand in the doorway for a moment before heading over to an available bar stool at the corner. I order a local beer and settle into my spot. It is not very crowded, making it easy to scan the various tables. Suddenly, like a flash of lightning, I spot a gorgeous femme sitting on a stool at the opposite end of the bar. She is laughing and joking with the bartender. I feel like I know her, like I've seen her somewhere before, when it strikes me. I watch her sip her drink. Yes, it is her, I decide. I remember that she appeared in a lesbian sex show in Seattle about a year ago. I don't know her real name, but I remember her stage name is Mona Delight. She was my favourite performer of the night, and after the show, I had spoken to her. I take a deep breath for courage, pick up my beer bottle, slip off my bar stool, and go over to her.

"Hi, I'm Casey ... from Vancouver. We've met before ... in Seattle, at the sex show at The Wild Rose...."

She looks me up and down, giving me the once over, her eyes twinkling, the corners of her mouth breaking into a smile, as if she is pleased with what she sees.

"Oh yeah," she says, "I remember. You're that cute Jewish butch. You were there with your girlfriend."

"Yeah," I say, happy she remembers, "that's right."

"Are you still with her?"

"Not tonight."

She raises her eyebrows at me.

"Can I buy you a drink?" I ask.

"Why not?" she responds. I signal to the bartender.

"One more of whatever she's drinking," I say. We drink our drinks and after a while I happily realize that she is trying to charm me just as much as I am trying to charm her. We talk about sex and dykes and San Francisco and Vancouver and sex and women and butch and femme and leather and sex. I am getting hotter by the minute. I feel my cunt getting slippery inside my pants and we talk about sex some more. I decide that it's time to get bold.

"You sure are one hot woman," I flatter her. "We could sure have a real nice time together ... if we were alone."

"Oh yeah?" she teases me, grabbing the scruff of my jacket in her fist, pulling me in close and holding on tight. "What exactly do you have in mind?"

"Well," I continue, our lips mere inches apart, "first I'd like to kiss you, deep and long and hot. I'd kiss you so good you'd almost come."

Her deep brown eyes penetrate into mine. I can see her getting aroused. She leans in closer to me, rubbing her leg up against mine.

"And then what would you do?" she asks.

"I would unlace that lacy shirt of yours, slowly, and I would hold your tits in my hands and play with your brown nipples..."

She flashes her eyes at me and moans softly.

I reach for her hand and bring it inside my jacket, so she can feel the dildo I have concealed in my secret pocket. I can see in her eyes that she is intrigued. She fondles my toy and then moves her hand around to pinch my nipple between her thumb and forefinger. I gasp.

"I think we should go somewhere else," she says.

"Like where?" I ask, ready to melt to her every demand.

"Like my place," she answers, twisting my nipple harder.

"Great," I say, and we waste no time in leaving the bar. When we get to her place, we shut the door behind us. We embrace instantly, hungry for each other. I take her face in my hands and kiss her. She kisses me back, ramming her tongue into my mouth, searching for the taste of me. She rips my jacket off and removes her own. I lower the thin strap of her top. She lets me. I play with her breasts. She loves it. She starts to unsnap my chaps and then pushes them down to the floor. I try to get them all the way off but trip on them, knocking us over onto the carpet. I go to remove her panty hose and discover that she is wearing old-fashioned stockings with a seam up the back, held up on her thighs by garters. This turns me on immensely.

She unbuttons my 501's and unhooks my belt. My safe sex pouch slips off and into her hand.

"What's this?" she asks.

"Standard equipment," I answer.

She opens the main snap and looks inside. "You come prepared," she says.

"Or I don't come at all," I can't resist saying.

"I'm impressed," she says.

"You ain't seen nothing yet," I say back, as I push her black leather skirt up over her pelvis. I discover to my pleasure that she is not wearing any panties. "Oh," I say, "you were expecting me tonight."

"Or someone like you," she answers.

I kiss her again, fiercely this time, as if I could take her inside of me. We are sweating. Our cunts are dripping. We are happy and horny and ready for each other. From outside, we can hear a car drive by, its stereo blaring. We thrash around, on top of and inside of each other. I am on top of her. She is on top of me. Nothing else matters but this moment, this place, as we ride off into the night, two women, lots of leather, lube, and latex, two hot bodies, and all the time in the world.

Heartbeat

MONA OIKAWA

For Leslie Komori,
Sansei sister, who was the first
to show me the power and meaning of taiko.

My silent yearning in summer's heat has once again led me to Michigan. Settled comfortably on my air mattress and down sleeping bag, I wait for Emi to return from her morning jog. All I can think about is how I love taiko drumming. The rhythms play fire, touching off embers of historic remembrance inside of me, igniting feelings that lie dormant and dry. They speak to my heart. "They are like a heartbeat," my taiko sisters tell me.

At each taiko performance, I feel the roar of drums, beginning in my chest under my ribs. Vibrations flowing in fiery waves, joining the world through my circling arms and stomping feet.

"You sure get into this stuff," a white woman once said to me.

"In my opinion, it's even better than k.d. lang," I answered, ignoring her astonished stare.

The urge to hear taiko music sometimes strikes me at unpredictable moments. If it hits me late at night and I'm alone, I lie in bed with my walkperson on and listen to the latest tape by Uzume Taiko. There have been other times, in the presence of a special friend, where wearing headphones would have been perceived as anti-social; yet, I have been overcome with the need to hear that familiar, comforting heartbeat.

"I don't know whether it's me who makes you come, or that damn taiko music you insist on playing as erotic accompaniment," one of my lovers joked after a particularly stimulating love-making afternoon.

Women always ask me why I don't join the Toronto taiko group. "I'm too busy with political commitments," I have replied, usually changing the subject without pause. Actually, the truth lies in scar tissue hidden in the crease of my left shoulder and in my doctor's warning, "You don't want to spend another six weeks in a body cast. And besides," he added, "I thought only men played those Japanese drums."

Little does he know, I thought to myself, pulling on my t-shirt and jumping off the examination table. I remember feeling that there had to be another way to recover from my injury. Outside the hospital door, I opened the garbage can, tossed in the prescription for anti-inflammatories, and pretended I was a muscular taiko sister as I pounded the lid with my umbrella.

"Deep in thought?" Emi enters the tent in her typical dramatic style. "We have to practice for the night stage performance. There's always so little time to talk to you when you come to see us at Michigan. How's your research going anyway?"

"It's going to be a long haul tracing the historic roots of taiko and analysing its regeneration by Canadian taiko groups within an Asian feminist context," I answer in a rather loud voice. That Emi, always asking for an update on my 'research.' I may even have to write something down to show her next time.

You see, even more than taiko drumming, I love taiko drummers, particularly of the female persuasion. Being a Japanese Canadian feminist historian gives me the cover I need to be a taiko groupie. And this year's Michigan Womyn's Music Festival offers an excellent setting in which to gather more data on my favourite all-woman taiko group.

"You might want to interview Midori, our newest member. She's living in Vancouver but was born in Hawaii." Emi is staring at my empty notebook. "You've interviewed the rest of us, I don't know how many times already! Midori's a massage therapist; she has incredible hands."

"Is she the woman wearing the white lace ... top?" I ask, pretending to jot down items in my notebook.

"So, you've noticed." Emi smiles broadly. "I have to go now. I'll introduce you at dinner."

Noticed is an understatement. Their new member is absolutely gorgeous. I had seen her at the women of colour tent, wearing bright red pants that were covered in a sea of playful fish swimming in folds around her legs. She walked, comfortably clothed in the crowd of naked women, her white camisole attracting more of my attention than any of the bare and burning cleavage around me.

I, on the other hand, am feeling quite self-conscious in my wild assortment of feminist t-shirts. Although I've started weight training as part of my new drug-free therapy, I'm not ready to unleash my budding biceps on these hungry Michigan women. And there is still the scar that I haven't revealed, even to some of my lovers.

"Elizabeth, this is Midori." Emi winks in my direction.

"I'm very happy to meet you," I answer, as I fill my plate with salad.

"I heard you are doing research on taiko." Midori looks intently as I pull out my notebook.

"Yes. If you have a minute, I'd really like to interview you." I try to swallow the food caught in my throat.

"Of course. But I really want to talk to you about what we're organizing in Vancouver for next year." Midori is sitting cross-legged, the black pupils of her eyes focused on mine as she speaks.

"As you know, 1992 is the fiftieth anniversary of the internment of Japanese Canadians. So we want to gather as many people of Japanese origin together as possible on the west coast. We're calling it the HomeComing. In Japanese, it's bokyo, yearning for home." Midori looks away for a second and her eyes fill with tears. "I didn't even know Japanese Canadians were interned until I moved to Vancouver last year. But then I've met Japanese Americans who didn't know that some people were taken from their homes in Hawaii and imprisoned on the mainland. My grandfather worked for a Japanese language newspaper in Honolulu and all of his family were shipped to the Manzanar prison camp."

I am feeling the fires of raging memory erupting inside of me. And it is not the taiko drums that are the connection to my heart this time; it is seeing this passionate, gentle woman's face moving with remembering. "My parents were born on the west coast." She leans closer to me, listening. "In a world where home doesn't really exist, I sometimes dream that maybe Vancouver could be a home for me. My grandmother's house, stolen from her by the government, is still standing in the Fraser Valley and I have this fantasy that I will take it back some day. But I didn't know people of Japanese origin in Hawaii were imprisoned. I guess we have a lot to learn about each other. I mean ... all women of colour have so much to learn about each other's histories."

"Maybe you could give a talk on your research. You must have a lot of material." She is looking at me seriously.

"I don't know if I'm ready to present it yet." In the face of her warm sincerity, I feel like a fraud. "Let me think about it."

"It may be healing for you to come back to the coast. Kaerimasu ka? We can talk more tomorrow," she says. "Maybe after the taiko workshop. I have to dress now for the night performance." She touches my arm and is gone.

I am looking at the sky growing dark with night. I make my way toward the stage, take a front row spot, try to listen to the performers. Relax. I worry that my heart will take flight and carry me away even before the drums begin. Crushes on taiko drummers were always okay, but this feels different. It is against my lesbian ethics to get hung up on anyone, I remind myself, particularly someone who lives thousands of miles away.

Women are setting up the stage for the taiko set. Maybe I should go back to my tent. There is still time. I could even drive home early tomorrow. Leave the sisters a note saying I wasn't feeling well.

Suddenly, the sound of the shakuhachi chases my doubts into clouds of yearning. I watch Sun-ja move fingers deftly across the bamboo instrument. My sisters' arms are raised and I know their bachi will soon hit the drumskins. I see their rippling muscles, Asian women powerful and proud, pouring out our histories, every movement a choreography of time and telling. I try not to look at Midori, but my eyes move toward her, helpless in their wanting, answering to her heartbeart, waves of joy carry me breathless to my feet.

Thunderous sparks fly toward the sky above this women's gathering. I feel strong to see my sisters shouting, dancing, crying, whispering, pounding. They are telling the story of people we love being forced into prison camps. The past is always in our present; women of colour know this. Tears are flowing fast as rapids in a river. I am shouting. Sisters of colour are at my side embracing, arms entwining.

My sisters wave as women shout for encores. They are exhausted, but I see their pleasure in knowing they were together in rhythm and strength. Morning, and their workshop will come quickly. They will rest now.

As the sun rises bright over the horizon, I decide I will not leave. I must talk with her again. I want to see her face brilliant with life on this last day at Michigan.

Midori comes toward me. "Nice t-shirt you have on."

"Thanks." I am trying not to look at her white camisole, her breasts etching prominent dark brown patches beneath the fragile lace.

"Can you help me set up the drums?" she asks, moving toward the biggest one.

"I can't," I stammer slowly. "I've had surgery on my shoulder and I'm not supposed to lift things, heavy things."

"I didn't know," she says with compassion.

"Not very many women do," I answer. "I guess I've been embarrassed about it."

"Maybe I can work on your shoulder before we leave tomorrow. I want to talk more with you about your research and about coming to Vancouver. Can we have dinner?"

"I would love to," I answer.

My cast iron teapot is steaming with kukicha on the gas camp stove outside my tent. "I can't wait to get home and cook some rice," Midori says, placing her fork on her plate. "What do you think about coming to Vancouver?"

"Well, I really don't know if I have anything of great importance to say about taiko. I think the power is in your performing it. I just say I'm doing research, so I can hang out with taiko players. It's the next best thing to drumming, I guess."

"Emi did make a joke about how you are her favourite notebook-carrying groupie." Midori's smile widens, emphasizing the dimple in her right cheek.

"But I think you should come anyway. It would be fun to get to know you better. I want women's voices heard there. Lots of Nikkei women's voices from across the country."

My heart is becoming less guarded, opening to the passion in her words. "Well, I was thinking last night, as I stood watching you, ahh ... as in you, the group; there were so many women of colour who gathered beside me. Taiko brought us together. I thought maybe we could do that in Vancouver. Get women of colour together to talk about how we survive. Play music, tell stories."

Midori's eyes are shining with excitement. "Yes. Next year is the 500th anniversary of the resistance of First Nation's peoples to the invasion of their land. This is a time for us to honour the struggles of the past. We could come together at the HomeComing to talk about how women of colour can continue to resist racism and all the shit that we face."

I move closer to her in the fading light, so as not to lose sight of her face, intense with hope and dreaming. My voice takes on a softness, revealing a part of me often hidden from the world. "That would be so wonderful. I really feel this is the only way we will survive: we need to work together as women of colour. And although we grieve the way our people were treated and robbed of our property, we know that the land had already been stolen by white people from the first peoples on this earth. There have been so many losses, before and after ours."

"Can I borrow some paper from your notebook?" Midori asks.

"You can have it," I smile shyly. "I'm really glad I met you."

"Me too," she answers. She touches my arm but this time keeps her hand lightly resting on my skin. "There's a drumming conference in Ottawa in the fall. Maybe we could meet and do more planning. You'd have a lot more women to interview there."

"If I came, I'm not sure I'd want to be with other women," I answer.

"I'll work on your shoulder now, if you want," she says. Her hand has moved upward and is firmly on my arm. "Your shoulder muscles are quite strong."

The skin beneath her hand is glowing, vibrations flowing in fiery waves. I try to speak through quickening pulse and breath. "I have been weight training for a few months."

"I know some exercises you could do. If I give you a routine, I would want to check on your progress from time-to-time." She moves behind me, fingering my shoulders, finding old wounds, healing the pain.

"You know, I have a scar from the surgery." The air is pounding with my heartbeat. "Would you like to see it?"

"Take off your t-shirt," she whispers. "I really hope you will come to Vancouver next year." Midori's hands are on mine, gently moving my shirt above my head.

"Yes. I will try. I think I'm ready now. *Kaerimasho*."

Nikkei: people of Japanese origin
kaerimasu ka: will you come home?
kaerimasho: let's go home

Coin Operator

LOVIE SIZZLE

The chocolate stains on the lapels of my chenille robe remind me of the hot date I had with the shortstop last spring. This starts me fantasizing about sex, fantasizing about sex with Dale Evans — she is singing to me as her lariat wraps around the fender of my convertible. But alas, this is only a fantasy, I am alone.

One of the things I often do when I'm alone and in need of a little racy romance is to press up against the Maytag during the Spin cycle. (The lipstick marks wipe off the enamel real easy and you don't have to worry about batteries.)

Sometimes I become adventurous and take my fantasies to town. I cruise the laundromats. I dress up real special, frequently opting for the velvet western shirt with the Holstein naugahyde fringe. I splash on a little Old Spicette cologne, get a nice pointy beehive happening, top it off with a plaid hairnet, and I know I'm ready for love. I kickstart the Dodge, slap in an Ethel Merman tape, and leave the trailer court in a cloud of dust.

I cruise past the laundromat of choice a few times and I park the car down the street. It's a hot night in the city. Pools of sweat form beneath the elastic tops of my patterned knee highs. I stroll up the block, drawn in by the neon sign flashing "Drop Your Load Here."

Standing tall in the doorway, fondling the roll of quarters in my pocket, I look over all the possibilities lined up, waiting. I know they are not looking forward to going through the Spin cycle all alone. I check them out. Some have seen better days, with lots of mileage on them, dents, rust, leaks, but what character, what stories they could tell. Ah, my gaze travels to the new ones, the neophytes, gleaming, beckoning, balanced and fast! Tonight there's even a Speed Queen available, but I'll avoid her — too many features, too experienced. I'll move in on the Sears or the Kenmore, a solid choice that's guaranteed to please.

I don't waste time with the bulletin boards or the video machines. I walk right up, without the security of a laundry basket, introduce myself, stroke the knobs a bit first, then drop in the quarters. I set the mood dials for Heavy Duty. If I was a little tired, it might be a Wash n' Wear night. None of the Delicate cycle stuff for me. I would never lift the lid; I don't want to become personally involved. I'm not into commitment.

She gets turned on real easy. Soon she is wet and agitated. Time seems to pass slowly, but we both know what we're here for. Finally I hear the beloved 'click' and my knees get weak. With the moaning sound of shifting gears and untethered desire that seems to come from deep down inside her, the Spin cycle starts! "Hold on honey," she seems to say. My thighs tremble as I try to grip the strong smooth sides, my palms wet with anticipation. She pounds against me with a strength that seems as if she could walk right through me. The sound of our passion thunders in my ears and seems to fill the room. Time has no measurement. Behind my tightly closed eyes, the darkness is invaded with waves of pleasure as she thumps and wheezes. Nothing short of a power failure could stop us now. I resist anticipating how this moment will end as the pinnacle of our lust moves closer to becoming a memory. Will the cycle stop abruptly? Or will we slowly grind to a halt with a hearty shudder?

I am just getting my focus back and adjusting my fringe when I hear ... another click. My God, she's wet again! Do I have what it takes to go through this a second time? Perhaps I'll leave now. Maybe I'll come back another night. Maybe she'll be here or maybe I won't care. I'll find another willing date silently waiting, or being so bold as to have her lid open.

I shine the toes of my boots with a discarded static cling-free cloth and head for the door. On my way out, I glance at the bulletin boards, resisting the urge to sign the petitions. I pause to light a cigarette in the doorway. The pulsing neon illuminates the glowing ash. With a sigh intertwined in a stream of exhaled smoke, I lean against the parking meter. Staring up at the steam filled windows, I reel with a feeling of satisfaction. Yet I am gripped with a sense of longing, knowing I'll never stay the night or take her to my cousin's wedding.

Pools of Heat

DIANE CARLEY

The warmth of the evening clung to me like stale cigarette smoke from the night before. Entering the familiar doorway, the cool darkness swept the heat away like a fan blowing dust across an empty floor. A steady thump of music rushed up to greet me as I headed towards the lonely light that hung above a mirror, illuminating my approach.

Leaning against the bar, I ordered a soda and lime. It tasted white and harsh and burned with a sharp relief. The heat that had soaked through my skin resurfaced as the shimmering perfume of my sweat.

I rubbed the back of my hand across my forehead, and with one foot propped against the rung of my stool, I looked into the darkness around me. As the curved shadows slowly became women, I felt the weight of the city slip from my shoulders like rain off a slanted roof.

I leaned back against the bar as the music pulsed, as the taste of sex played across my lips, and my sleeping senses wakened. I swallowed the rest of my drink, savouring the scent of sweet danger that permeated this safe place. Turning to the mirror, I ordered another drink.

"Do you wanna dance?" a voice behind me asked.

I saw the surprised look on my face, felt the space between us pressing against my back. I stood still for a moment, enjoying its subtle suggestion. Then I turned around and smiled.

"Sure," I said.

We headed towards the tangle of bodies beating time against each other. She began to move slowly to the music. I fell into the mirror of her motions and we held each other's gaze as our bodies rode the rhythm of the song.

Her movements sent feather blows of desire striking hard against my gut. I countered with my own and smiled as I saw them hit their mark. We struck and parried and danced the shadow box dance while music swirled around us and welts of passion began to rise in our eyes.

Then the music changed and so did our dance. All that we had thrown at each other settled back into the quiet place between us, became part of the embrace we entered. I laid my arms around her neck and let my fingertips dangle across her shoulders.

She held me at a distance, her hands a gentle weight on the small of my back. I wanted to be close; I needed to feel the pressure of her open fists on my waist. But she barely touched me as I followed her and the invisible string connecting us, pulling whenever, whichever way she tugged. We moved in tandem, a synchronized swim across the dance floor.

She pulled me to her, the softness of her breasts against mine cutting a brittle edge through the delicate flesh of my belly. Then she stepped back, my stomach falling through the fragile hole. I tried to draw close, to seal up this wound, but she shifted past me.

She commanded my body, her hands barely touching my back, while I pursued, seeking the relief of her touch. Then she stopped. We stood, barely in each other's arms, as a frenetic movement surged all around us. Everyone was moving to the beat of the music while I stood captive in her stillness.

"Come home with me," she said.

"All right," I replied.

We walked to the door. Outside, the stagnant air hung like pools of heat from the gently darkening sky. Together we stepped into the moist heaviness of the early evening and headed towards her car. We got in and she started to drive. Gusts of wind blew hair off my face as we drove through the empty streets. I looked at her in the purple light of the fading day and felt a hand squeezing my heart. I turned away.

She drove the car into a driveway, got out, and headed towards the house. I hurried after her. We stepped inside and she turned to me. She reached out and stroked my face. Her hand slid down my cheek to my neck, under the collar of my shirt, while her other hand began a gentle journey down my body, leaving a line of startled flesh in its wake.

Then she held my face and I felt her warm breath as she brought her lips to mine. I closed my eyes. She undid the top button of my shirt, working her way downwards, slowly releasing each one.

Her dry, warm hands glided over my back and chest as my body strained towards her. Her fingers slid over my nipples, barely making contact, but igniting a fierce tremor in me. It wasn't just my body she excited, everything within me dripped at the hint of her touch.

I felt the pain, the empty, aching spaces wherever her hands were not. I could not even summon the strength to touch her. My hands lay limp at my side as hers fluttered over my skin.

She stroked my stomach where my flesh ended and my jeans began. She undid my button and pulled the zipper down. I felt the heat from her hands as they travelled over the denim hugging my skin.

She started to pull down my jeans as she kissed and caressed my newly exposed flesh. She took the band of my underpants in her teeth, wrenched it away from my skin, and let it snap back.

She was on her knees in front of me, tongue and lips playing over my naked skin. She started to tug on my pants which still clung to my cunt. I felt the cool air pour over the pain of my wetness. She kissed my stomach and legs, running her hands over my body. Finally, she slipped my pants off and stood up to lift the shirt from my shoulders.

I felt a chill from the sweat of my body mingling with the heavy summer air. She stood in front of me fully clothed. I shut my eyes to hide my own nakedness but opened them as she brought her face once again towards mine. She kissed me on the lips, stepped back, and began to take off her clothes.

I watched as she undid the buttons of her shirt, caressing herself, slowly, sensually, her eyes closed and her head tilted back in pleasure. She slipped off her pants, gently, taunting me with what she witheld from me. She teased me with what I couldn't see, what I couldn't touch.

I wanted to touch but didn't dare. Naked, she stepped closer and took me into her arms. I melted into the feel of her skin against mine, succumbing to the blistering sensation shooting through my veins.

I was torn between surrendering completely to her touch and thrusting my body hard against hers. I grasped her face and kissed her. A sheet of intensity covered us both, until, needing to breathe, I pushed her away. She took my hand and led me upstairs to the bed.

She pulled me down on top of her. It was as if I had never felt her body before. We both started to move. Together our bodies caressed each other, using everything but our hands. Then tongues and hands and lips and fingers ran rampant over breasts and bellies and backs and mouths, clutching, licking, sucking, holding, till we collapsed, spent and aching, tied up in each other's arms.

"So what did you say your name was?" she asked.

"Very funny Joanne."

She rolled over on top of me and I felt it beginning again. After five years together, her seductions ran deeper and harder than ever before. When she touched me, it was as if she ignited a hundred tiny lights all over my body, creating an intricate pattern of complex love. Each time was different, but the colours of the years created explosions brighter and fuller than the intense white light of young love.

At one time, a mere touch of her hand was enough to send me spiralling down into the core of my feeling. The journey was a different one now, slower, more thorough, touching places skipped over during the hasty passion of those early years.

I had no desire to return to that wet, sloppy high of dancing inside an unknown fire. I preferred the body that knew mine intimately, completely, playing me with the sensitivity and instinct of an accomplished musician. I trusted those hands, allowing her to draw from me the melodies nobody else ever had.

I slid my hands down her salty, slippery back, the feel of her body on mine, pushing me past the limits of desire, straight into raw, throbbing need. It mounted in me like a sweet, heady dream, ready to spill into her arms.

Afterwards, we lay on our backs, beside each other. We held hands as the cool night breeze blew through the open window, caressing our tired bodies.

"How do you do what you do to me after all this time?" I asked. "No, don't answer, I don't want to know. Just promise you'll never stop doing it."

"I promise," she said. "Now go to sleep. We've both had a full day ... and night."

She kissed me gently and turned on her side to sleep. I curled up behind her, held her tightly, determined never to let her go. I closed my eyes and felt the love in her touch I remembered so well, the touch in her love.

POEM FOR PAT
\on seeing an o'jays concert in buffalo

KAREN AUGUSTINE

Dark skin
sweats in a string of beads
red
green
black
on my neck
Your tongue
       tasty   touching
caught between my teeth
caresses the roof of my mouth
3 times

                this is all about wanting your mouth
                on my klit.
                              deep.
                pushing your tongue in me.

it has to do with my hands up your
shirt. stroking your breasts.
gasping for breath/

pressing you up against
a wall
trying to fit my thigh
between your legs
to pressure
just the right spot.

Brown Brown
hands
catch in the kink
of my hair
hug the mound between my legs
grip the dampness
that is white

you feel sticky sticky
wet
on my fingers.

i mumble mucous on my mouth/
you taste
like honey
love
gone to heaven
and i just want
to get
you out of
those clothes
so we
can fuk.

I crave your mouth/muscle
against my thigh
plunging to the back of my throat
stabbing the nerve of my lower back

       naked and warm. your body sweat strokes mine/
          slide
          slick
          slapping skin

                 bodies
            tightly locked
       in the most unreal position i've ever
       imagined.

You shake me
by the skin
from the palm
of your hand
Make me kum twice
with the hardness
of your knee

       i can only scream. stroke your teeth with my tongue.
       grasp the side of your ribs. slide
       down
       the dampness
       of   your   back
                    and wait.

A Promise of Something

SUSAN J. FRIEDMAN

There are beautiful women everywhere, if you have the eyes to look for them. That summer, I did. Single and celibate for over a year, I was, physically and emotionally, as taut as a harp string waiting to be plucked. And yet, even when the opportunity presented itself, a curious reluctance outweighed my more elemental urges.

Yeah, I said to myself, it's called common sense.

I do that a lot — talk to myself, I mean. Silently, of course, so as not to end up in the loony bin. Or out loud occasionally, to my cat, Pooks, in the privacy of my own apartment.

As I carried on this inward dialogue, I was perched at the end of a row of orange plastic seats, at Continental Gate Number 42, Cleveland-Hopkins airport. My shoulder bag, stuffed to the gills with books, papers, and baked goods, rested firmly between my feet. This had been a mixed business and pleasure trip: business being a work-related conference, pleasure being a visit with an old and dear friend who lives in Cleveland Heights.

Spending time with my friend, Sarah, and her lover of five years, Janie, moved me to contemplate my own love-life. Or lack thereof. Sarah and Janie seemed so in love, so sane, so good for each other. We'd spent hours sipping iced coffee at Arabica, my favorite hang-out in Cleveland Heights, listening to Patsy Cline, while I lamented to Sarah about the trials and tribulations of singledom.

"I'm horny as hell," I told her, "and it's not like I haven't dated anyone..."

"So, *nu*, what happened?"

"Nothing," I concluded glumly, stirring half and half into my second glass of iced coffee mocha.

Sarah is a good friend. She didn't press me. She sat and waited until I was ready to tell her why. I sat and listened and began to sing softly with Patsy, "Crazy ... I'm crazy for feelin' so lonely..."

Thus fortified, I continued:

"Nothing happened because it just seemed too goddamned complicated. You know: either they wanted to get married, or I thought I did! Or they had some other lover and I felt too jealous. Once it was someone from work and I just thought, my god, no matter what happens, I'm going to have to pass her in the halls every day..." I threw up my hands in mock submission. "I guess I'm just not cut out for the casual affair!"

Sarah, the stinker, laughed at me. She knew what I was talking about though. She wasn't big on casual affairs either.

"I wish I was a gay man!" I blurted.

"Why?" Sarah looked at me challengingly. "You think they have it so easy?"

"Well, maybe not," I admitted reluctantly. "But the point is, I envy anyone, male or female, who can have casual liaisons without guilt. I mean: sex as bodily need. 'Skin hunger,' one of my friends calls it. You've got an itch, so scratch it."

"Don't despair yet, sweetie," Sarah admonished as we rose to go. "Your day will come!"

We continued the discussion later that day, while weeding Sarah's old fashioned flower beds.

"I'm just not *ready* yet!" I pronounced, simultaneously uprooting a stubborn dandelion.

"Watch the begonias," Sarah warned, adding, "Ready for what?"

I grinned. My remark was out of context. As usual, I'd continued an old conversation in my head and made the transition to out loud with no preliminaries. I tried to elaborate.

"Someday, I want to have something like what you and Janie have. But not now. I mean, I'm still not totally over Jill. That was ten years of my life."

Sarah paused in her weeding to face me. "Well, some say, to recover, it's one year for every year you've been in the relationship."

"That kind of encouragement I can do without, thank you very much," I muttered, glaring at my friend indignantly.

"You're welcome." Sarah smiled. "I don't really think it takes that long — but of course you're still grieving, *hubbeleh* — it's been less than a year."

"I know."

I let out a long sigh.

"The stupid thing is, I *like* being single in some ways. I really need this time. I'm getting to know myself, what I like, what I don't like. I know it sounds corny, but it's true."

"It's not corny at all and it is true. This year's been good for you, I can tell. But it's also true," she added, winking, "that you want to touch and be touched, and that your hormones are going just a little crazy. I mean, come on, you were lusting after Jessica Lange and Candice Bergen last night on TV!"

"So were you," I felt compelled to point out to her.

"Damn right I was! I may love Janie, but I'm not dead!"

I suppose I wished Sarah could solve something, fix something in my life to make it right. She couldn't. But in her warm hug goodbye at the Continental terminal, I felt all the years of our friendship like a shield and a strength, shoring me up for the rest of my life back home. I tried to believe what she'd said to me the previous day:

"When you're ready — no sooner, no later — the right woman will appear. And till then, you may yet have your casual affair; I did. Three weeks! And it was fun while it lasted!"

And so, sitting contemplatively at terminal 42, I resurrected one of my old, favorite pastimes: picking out the women I found most attractive.

At first, although there was quite a crowd, I didn't have much luck. Directly across from me was a spikey-haired blonde teenager wearing a sweatshirt from Hard Rock Cafe in Stockholm, deeply embedded in a Stephen King novel.

Too young, I wistfully concluded.

Two rows away, a young mother struggled with three small and whining children. Her face was taut with concentration, anxiety, and love.

Too distracted. Too unavailable, I thought.

My eyes scanned further, past business men with their brief cases and expensive suits, past a white-haired couple reading a travel guide to Boston.... Finally, I gave up the effort to find a nice woman to pin my fantasies on and turned to my murder mystery. I could, perhaps, fantasize that tough, sexy detective V.I. Warshawski was, in reality, a lesbian...

Two chapters later (leaving V.I. in a most precarious predicament), I felt someone looking at me. You know how you can just *feel* when someone's got their eye on you, but then you're too embarrassed to look up and see who it is? Or you think you're just imagining things? Well, that's how I felt. I tried to get back to my book, but the feeling of being watched persisted. Finally, I gave in to my curiosity and looked up.

Sitting two rows and a few seats away, in the spot previously occupied by the frazzled mother, was a woman I most assuredly had not seen before. I would've noticed. She looked down, it seemed, at the precise instant that I looked up; yet I had the feeling that she was doing it on purpose, letting me get a good look without feeling too embarrassed.

Now, this is going to sound a little weird, but to this day I can't describe her exactly. Certain details seem to change every time I recall her. I do know that the woman was enormously attractive; it seemed that I could feel her sexual energy twenty feet away, rising to meet my own, lingering and co-mingling in the air.

Sometimes when I remember her, she is wearing a soft, colorful dress, open at the throat, very feminine. Other times, I see her in tight jeans and a black tank top, her arms firm and muscular. Sometimes her hair is long and dark and wavy, like Amy Irving's in *Yentl*. Other times, it's short and dykey, cut to show off her face.

Always, I know that her eyes are grey: a beautiful kind of grey-flecked-with-blue that I'd not seen before and haven't seen since. Always, I know she was that blend of softness and strength that so attracts me in women.

I looked down.

And I felt her looking at me again. Looking me up and down. Looking clear inside. I looked up. And saw her tracing in the air with one long, delicate finger … something … some sign. Absurdly, it made me think of witches and hexes; I shook myself, thinking I must be imagining the whole thing.

Then, quite suddenly, she was beside me, in the chair next to mine, making ordinary conversation.

"I saw you reading," she almost purred, low voiced. "It does my heart good to see someone enjoying Sara Paretsky."

The sound was all cool greens, warm reds, and purples, and it made my heart beat in my cunt, I wanted her so bad.

To myself I was saying, This is ridiculous — she's just being friendly — you're in an *airport*, for god's sake! Yet I wanted to kiss her, right there, in front of all those people, without even knowing her name.

Aloud, I said, "It's my first time reading her. A friend lent this to me…and I love V.I. Warshawski, she's really something else…"

The woman nodded, all the time looking at me in a way that turned my whole body hot with desire. My nipples were hard and straining to leave my blouse ... my cunt was rising like a sweet baking cake ... I said, "My name is Judy."

She said, "My name is Ruth, and I want you too." And with her beautiful hand she was again tracing a sign in the air and right after that she began kissing me.

When we kissed, there was nothing. Nothing but her soft, strong tongue exploring inside me exploring inside her. Sometimes, she stopped and took my hand and gave small, soft kisses inside my moist palm, on each knuckle, down each finger, and then took my fingers into her mouth, sucking them gently.

Once, I pulled back and looked around wildly and she pulled me back saying, "Shhh, it's okay darlin', they can't see us." With my eyes, I followed her gaze and saw that it was true. I saw the Hard Rock Cafe girl still reading her novel, eating peanuts, one of the business men pacing back and forth in front of the long window, the older couple sharing an RC cola, all as if in a haze, voices muffled, and in complete oblivion to Judy and Ruth making love right in the middle of terminal 42.

Again, Ruth pulled me back to her and we began the ritual of unbuttoning, unfastening, unbosoming, pulling over, pulling off, pulling closer, and pulling back again, each to gaze upon the other. A process of discovery. A process of immense satisfaction in itself, punctuated by soft fingered touches, small delighted kisses, and loud noisy sucks and moans that no one heard but ourselves.

I barely noticed how we made our way from the sticky plastic seats, down to the carpeted floor, or how Ruth produced a soft black blanket, spread it for us in what used to be the aisle.

My intensity built. I wanted to pull Ruth on top of me, to feel her large breasts cascading over me, her warm belly brushing my warm belly, her strong thigh clamped between my own two thighs (it had been so long!); I wanted to roll on top of her, press deep into her, let her take my two rosebud nipples at once in her mouth, let her feel the heat of my cunt, feeling the heat of her cunt, let her feel my mouth my teeth my tongue tasting and probing, down

down inward inside where it's wet and dark and silken, let those beautiful hands slide down into around under between. I wanted to look into those eyes, looking back into mine, calling Ruthie, calling Judy, as if we'd always known this...

And I did and we did, all this and more besides.

"All passengers for flight number 660 to Boston, please look at your boarding passes at this time. Those passengers with seat numbers..."

The high, thin whine of the terminal speaker pierced our quiet holding of one another. Silently, slowly, we pulled apart.

"Your flight," Ruth whispered, as we each pulled on our clothes.

"Yes," I whispered back to her.

Then she kissed me, a soft, quiet, passionate kiss that was like the promise of something.

And when she was gone, I picked up my shoulder bag and my murder mystery, and I headed for the gate.

Nu: a yiddish word meaning "So?" or "Well now"
Bubbeleh: a yiddish endearment

A Horny Corny Story

JAN

Literature Test — Instructions
Read the following story carefully before answering the multiple-
choice questions at the end. Do not write on this test booklet. Use
the paper provided by the amazon monitors. Take as much time as
you need to complete this test.

A Horny Corny Story
The afternoon heat reminds her of having her face in a
woman's pussy. So humid and muffling is the heat that it
stifles her breath. She notes the many people shopping in
the market, enjoying the unexpected heat, and she wonders
why more of them aren't at home having sex. Warm
063   weather pressing in around her makes her horny.

She remembers the times she's had sex in this kind of
heat. After just a few minutes, the wetness that's sweat and
the wetness that's sweet woman's juices become a lovely
slippery mix. Then there are the ice cubes. She's never
quick enough with them and they melt before she's moved
them down the other woman's back, from the space between her shoulder blades to the smooth spread of her ass.
When there are only a few cool drops left on her fingertips,
she strokes the other women's asshole so she can hear her
161   say, "Oh yes, that feels nice."

She senses a wetness rippling out from deep inside her cunt and quickly checks her shopping list to distract herself. Just one more item to buy: corn. Soon she'll be at home, sitting in the artificial breeze of her oscillating fan, with a sweating glassful of cold water to alternately drink and

217 press to her forehead.

Sitting at home, she remembers how her grandmother used to roast corn for her and her cousins when they were kids. Her grandmother would pull the smoke-grey cobs off the rack, mere inches from the hot coals. She would juggle them in her brown palms and blow on the kernels before breaking the cobs in halves and giving them to the children

286 who squatted in the dirt around the fire pit.

When the remembering passes, she goes to the kitchen to cook the corn she has bought.

She marvels at how much the hairy end of the corn's protective husk looks and feels like pubic hair as she tugs it back to expose ripe bulbous kernels. She loves corn but hates the sinewy hairs she must pull from between her teeth after eating. She washes the cobs with cold water, shakes them, smells their freshness, and prepares to boil them until

371 they are bright and juicy.

The cooked cobs are so hot they would probably burn even her grandmother's old, leathery hands. She melts butter on two, sprinkles them with salt, and puts one cob aside. With loud smacking noises, she eats the buttered and

419 salted two. She strokes the bare and cooling cob.

As dusk pushes the day's sultry heat aside, she undresses and returns to the kitchen for the lone cob. She carries it to an armchair, sits, spreads her legs comfortably, and plays the cool cob around her dark pussy. Her lips immediately glisten with her own sticky wetness. She teases the cob slowly in and out of her cunt. First putting the slender end in just a bit, then easing its thick middle halfway into

534 herself, before slipping in its entire length, save for the small portion she grasps with her fingers. She sways her hips to the rhythm of her slow fucking motion.

With her other hand, she presses and squeezes her firm clit. She tightens her legs around the cob and feels cool liquid bursting from the kernels, mixing with her own juices to run down her thighs, into the crack of her raised ass. The walls of her pussy tighten, grab, and push for release. She throws her head back and cries out as she comes with the
600 fresh, sweet corn nestled inside her cunt.

Questions

To test your understanding of this story, choose a response for the following questions from the multiple-choice answers listed. Answers for questions 1–6 are worth 13.5% each. Question 7 requires an essay answer worth 19% of the test total.

1. Choose the phrase that best characterizes the tone of this story.
(a) playful erotic mush (b) offensive pornographic smut
(c) passionate meat-less fantasy (d) feverish hot weather hallucination

2. Identify the vegetable dildo in this story.
(a) cucumber (b) carrot (c) corn on the cob (d) celery (e) canned corn

3. Identify all sites of sexual or culinary encounter.
(a) market (b) bedroom (c) kitchen (d) living room

4. Identify all climactic moments in this story.
(a) while the protagonist does her grocery shopping (b) when she peels the corn (c) when she has an orgasm (d) when she eats the corn

5. Choose the best description of the main sexual activity in this story.
(a) tactile grain sex (b) dildo masturbation (c) unprotected corn fucking (d) boring non-sex activity

6. Identify the epicure protagonist in this story.
(a) a cook (b) a lesbian (c) any woman (d) a vegetarian

7. Choose an answer for the following question and write a 100-word essay explaining your choice. Would you like to know the woman in this story?
(a) No way. Never. (b) I do know her. (c) I am her. (d) She lives next door.

Reading Between the Lines

KIMBERLY-LEI MISTYSYN

She's beautiful, I think to myself as I gaze at her over a stack of books. She says she depends too much on cosmetics and has yet to see a decent photograph of herself. All I see in her is beauty, kindness, generousity, good judgment and a warm laugh. I can tell she is suffering from one of her migraines today. I find I often get headaches just from seeing her suffer. Wishful thinking, that I might be able to relieve her pain.

She's typing cards for new books and I yearn to reach over to caress her shoulder. A small sign to show I care. I'm certain, however, that were I to touch her she would sense my love and pull away. I once confessed my love to her in a letter. She tried to convince me that I saw her as a mother-figure and if I didn't get over my crush, I'd better walk out of her life immediately. She's married and I suppose I should see that as a barrier, but I cannot understand how she can ignore the depth of love I feel for her. I've worked as a volunteer for her in the library for almost eleven of my twenty-one years. She never questions my devotion. She's simply glad for the help. Somehow I hope she'll become so grateful for my help that someday she'll pay me back with a kiss or more.... We have built a special relationship over the years. We've become close friends. I would do anything for her and she knows it. In return, she's been there whenever I needed to confide in her or ask her advice. Mixed in with my unconditional love for her is another element: lust.

Many a night I have spent dreaming of ways to seduce her or ways she might suddenly try to seduce me. I realize by now that the dreams may never materialize, but they do keep my fantasy life rich.

Mary finishes carding some new novels and takes a long sip of steaming tea. She looks up and catches me staring at her. Sometimes I challenge her with my gaze, but usually (I have this problem with blushing) I avert my eyes and get back to work. At the end of each day she offers me a drive back home. The trip to my apartment is always so full of friendly banter that I never want to arrive home. Inevitably we must say our goodbyes.

Today my lover, Miche, greets me at the front door with a lingering kiss. She knows about my attraction to Mary but does not feel threatened. She knows I value our relationship too much to have an affair. She also feels confident that Mary will never return my feelings. Through Miche, I have come to recognize that looking at other women can enhance the sex life in a relationship.

"Has she seduced you yet?" Miche teases me.

Naturally, Miche never expects me to say yes. Today I feel like teasing her back. "Actually, I seduced her. Sit down and I'll tell you all about it."

The pink of my cheeks gives the tease away, but Miche decides to play along. She is somewhat startled that her shy, moralistic lover would even think about infidelity. Feigning disbelief, her wide eyes seem to mirror a look of hurt, surprise, and a definite hunger for detailed explanation. She sighs and flops face down on the bed. I lie down beside her and wonder which fantasy seduction I'm going to dream up this time. I've never fantasized aloud before. In a husky voice, I begin to fabricate my story and because every atom of my being wishes it were true, the desire weighs down my words.

"I was feeling rather depressed today because Mary was feeling so sick. She had one of her migraines. I was doing the usual jobs she asks of me, watering the plants, feeding the fish and shelving books. I found her keys five times for her today. You know how she's always misplacing them. And I brought her a mug of tea just minutes before noon."

As I speak into Miche's ear, I begin to nibble on it between sentences. My hand massages her back and 'accidentally' unhooks her bra. Miche rolls onto her back and I pause to lift up her shirt. Like a magnet, my mouth is drawn to her nipples.

"Don't stop. What happened?" As much as Miche likes my warm mouth on her breast, she loves a good fantasy. I could see her imagining it, as if it were really happening.

"Okay, the library was empty and Mary had just locked the door for lunch as I brought her the mug of tea. She was frantically searching for her keys. As I walked around a bookshelf, I realized that she was about to collide into me. I swerved but couldn't avoid her. Hot tea landed all over my white turtleneck. Mary stared at my breasts through the wet top and suddenly cried 'Are you burnt?' She ran to the sink in her office to fill the mug with cold water and grabbed a sponge. She ordered me to take my top off so she could put a cold sponge on me. Luckily, the shirt had soaked in most of the heat. I enjoyed her sympathetic clucks at the sight of my slightly reddened back. There was nothing at all romantic about this predicament, but I wanted to take advantage of the situation. Just to be safe, Mary went to her first aid kit and pulled out some burn ointment. She began rubbing it on my neck, shoulders, and back. At first I thought it was my imagination, but she seemed to graze the sides of my breasts."

I stopped to graze Miche's breasts a few times for effect. Pulling and tugging at a nipple, Miche groaned softly. I smothered the sound with a kiss. Miche kissed back with a fierceness that told me her desire was growing. Abruptly, she pulled away. "Did she make a move on you?"

"Nothing like that. Actually, I made the move on her. I decided if I didn't do something drastic, she was going to put the ointment away, give me a clean shirt to borrow, and that would be the end of it. Instead, I turned onto my back and said, 'My front needs ointment more than my back does.' I did this so quickly, she had no time to avert her eyes and I watched her face as she stared. Finally, she made an embarrassed attempt to look away while tossing me the ointment and telling me to put it on myself.

Amazed at my bravery, I swiftly took hold of her wrists and placed both of her hands on my firm, round breasts. I told her it would ease the pain if she did it. Her face went scarlet, but I noticed that she did not pull away. I slowly sat up, her hands still on my breasts, and I touched her face with a warm hand: 'Mary, just let it happen this once. My body is hot all over and I need your body to help cool it down. Besides, I can tell that you're feeling something.'

She didn't know what to say and choked on her words. I put a finger on her lips and she stopped. Then I reached over and kissed her. It was an awkward kiss at first, because she was still in shock and uncertain as to what to do, but slowly her body responded. Her mouth opened to let my tongue in and her limp arms wound their way around my waist."

As I related this to Miche, we both shed our clothes and wound our arms around each other. I felt Miche's knee come up between my legs. It was becoming difficult to speak. My breath was coming faster, but I had to tell her the rest. I continued the story, rubbing my pelvis rhythmically against her leg.

"I slowly unbuttoned and removed Mary's shirt and bra as she knelt there, not knowing what was going to happen next. Her eyes watched as my head lowered to a spot between her breasts. I licked a path around each breast and watched her nipples stiffen. Mary seemed intrigued that another woman was causing her body to come alive. She finally spoke to me: 'It isn't fair of you to excite me like this when you can't fulfil me. I mean, you obviously don't have the proper ... equipment ... to finish what you started.'

I assured her that she was in for a surprise and I kissed a path down to her navel. I began to tug at her zipper with my teeth, but then I stopped and asked her to lie down. Now the two of us were on the carpeted floor, hidden by millions of books, with just our pants on. I lay my body directly atop hers and pressed my breasts into her breasts. My hand ran up her leg and sandwiched itself between her cunt and mine as I kissed her. She gasped into my mouth and her pelvis began to push up into mine. I could feel her wetness through her slacks. Leaving my hand there, unmoving, and simply kissing her, I waited for her to figure out what she wanted me to do. Her pelvic thrusts became increasingly demanding and suddenly her hand was on my ass, pushing me down harder onto her. I decided that she was ready and my hand pulled down her zipper. Without removing her slacks, my hand slipped inside and into her underwear. With a finger, I spread the wetness around, building the suspense. When she began to plead, I dipped a finger into her widened opening.

As I did this, I slipped my other hand into my own jeans and into my thicket. Mary was moaning that she wanted to touch me, so I took her hand, introduced it to my cunt, and let her explore."

"Stop a minute," Miche ordered. Both of us were glistening with sweat. Miche caressed my cunt and found it to be as wet as what I'd been describing to her. She leaned over and tasted the juice with her tongue. Licking and sucking, I moaned loudly, but just as I was about to come, she stopped. Placing her knee where her mouth had been, she ordered me to finish telling her the story. I began to speak in a frenzy.

"Mary was lightly kneading my clitoris and I was feeling on top of the world. I pulled my hand out of her slacks and brought it up to her mouth. She tasted herself and then kissed me as my wet hand moistened her nipples with her juices. I re-entered her, putting in two fingers, three, four, and then I pulled back out. She was wet enough to try for a whole fist. I licked my knuckles all over and rubbed her clit in a circular motion. Slowly her folds opened wide and sucked me in. I pulled her pants the rest of the way off and leaned down to lick her mound as my fist thrust up inside of her. Her legs wrapped around my head, and with a long wail and an arched back, she exploded."

I couldn't speak anymore. I was rubbing against Miche's pelvis, out of control. I began to moan and call out Miche's name to which she responded. Miche has the ability to get turned on by seeing and hearing my excitement. We always manage to come at the same moment, which is a very special feeling.

As we held each other, Miche said, "I just can't believe you acted on your feelings for her, and not even a thought for me." I knew that Miche was still teasing me, but I was tired.

"Miche, as much as I want to make love to Mary, you know I couldn't. None of what I told you actually happened. Besides, I came home wearing the same shirt I left with."

Miche, however, was not willing to let me get away with just falling asleep: "I haven't told you about my day yet. That professor I've been eyeing had lunch with me today. We both ate in her private office..."

Suddenly, I was wide awake and Miche was massaging my breasts. If it weren't for the grin I saw before she began kissing my neck, I might have believed her.

Sweet Meat

LOIS FINE

When I was six, my parents
marched me up the stairs,
into a hospital waiting room.
"And what seems to be the problem here?"
The doctor is a woman.
My mother shifts, my father speaks.
"We're here about her voice."
"I see."
I am looking at her stethoscope, her white coat with the hospital
stamp,
"Voice Pathology."
"Can you say Peter Piper Picked a Peck?"
I do and we all laugh.
"Will she need an operation, doctor?"
"No, I don't think that will be necessary. We'll try a few
exercises. I see what you mean though. Very low."
"Too low."
"Now, what's a pretty girl like you doing with your voice all the
way down in your stomach?"
We all laugh.
She shows me how to do the exercises.

I practise in front of her, carefully lifting my ear lobes up into
my ears, listening for my voice as she has shown me, repeating
very slowly in the highest voice I can find,
"Sweet meat.
Eat feet.
Neat seat.
Sweet meat."
"There, that's very good. Now you do that every day."
We all nod.
I am diligent, practising at home in the mirror.
"Hey Lois, want to come outside and play?"
"Soon, when I'm finished my exercises."
"Nah, nah, sweet meat, neat feet," and everyone has their ear
lobes turned inside out and everyone is laughing.
It works ... eventually.
My voice leaves my stomach and sits in my throat.
Higher, forced,
uncertain.
Should I say "properly" female?
Years later, I am in my lover's arms.
"You know, I really love your voice."
"You do?"
"Especially when you laugh, it's so low."
My throat tightens.
"And I love how deep your voice gets when you come. It's like
I'm hearing the real you."
And I reach for her then, pulling her down into me.
Her hands are strong and gentle finding their place inside me,
filling me up, uncovering my self.
I speak to her from my stomach now.
From my belly where I shake and rumble,
from my guts where I live.
Sweet meat, they said,
so that I would dance with boys and not with girls.

Sweet meat,
so that I would wear a dress.
Sweet meat,
and they stole my six-year-old lusty, gutsy voice.
I am in my lover's arms now and our hips move, grinding steady.
"Talk to me, baby," she says. "I love the sound of you."
She slips her fingers inside me.
"Talk to me," and I moan.
Her fingers inside me in and out and
Sweet meat,
and they thought that boys would turn my head.
Sweet meat,
and they thought that I would never hear past my ear lobes.
Sweet meat, and she is fucking me harder now, her hands never stop
and she loves it when I come.
"I love how you sound when you come. Your voice so deep and
so low. Talk to me," she says.
And I do.

Report to the Community

K.LINDA KIVI

Prologue: This report was commissioned by the Blackhurst lesbian community. Seven women to be more precise. We were sitting on Tiiu's front porch one evening, smoking pot, when they came up with the idea of getting someone to research the new woman in town. I was paying attention to my sore tooth when, suddenly, I became the focus for their scheme.

"But why me?" I had wanted to know. "I haven't even met the woman. Yet."

"Because you're good at research and you're single," Laura had answered.

I wagged my chin in Myla's direction, "What about her?"

Myla's if-only-you-knew, full tooth grimace read like a Naiad novel. She tipped her head in Claire's direction. Claire looked nervously at Sue (her primary lover) and Sue rolled her eyes. Sometimes this community nauseates me.

To lighten the tone, or perhaps make matters worse, Tiiu started singing "Monogamy, shpodogamy." Laura and Marg joined in with gusto. The trio shifted uncomfortably in their seats. I took pity.

"Ah ... so what about this report? Are you guys serious?"

"Time to get serious, is it?" Laura likes to be In Charge.

"Why don't we just invite her to dinner?" My tooth hurt. I wasn't in the mood for games.

"Just invite her to dinner? I can't believe you're not more interested." Myla obviously was.

Tiiu echoed her enthusiasm. "How often does a new woman show up in this backwater? When was the last time?"

"Two years ago?" someone muttered a guess.

"Besides, it takes forever to get to know someone over dinner. We don't want to have to wait for the juicy details." Tiiu was waving her hands around the way she does when she gets excited.

"Naaaah!" came the chorus from the rest. "We don't want to wait! Re-port! Re-port! Re-port!"

Oh no, I thought. They're serious. Shit.

"What about the ethics of paying someone to write a report about an unsuspecting woman?" I get philosophical when stoned. They seemed to get sillier and sillier. Why did I bother trying to reason with them?

"A hundred bucks," Laura answered, evading my question entirely. She looked at the others for approval and six heads seemed to bob.

"So you think you can get me to spy on some unsuspecting, and for all I know, uninteresting woman for money that you'll probably never pay me?"

I think the money was my undoing. Claire was the first to slap a five on the table. Tiiu followed suit with a ten. Crumpled bills piled up on the table before I could save myself.

Laura counted. "We've got fifty-three bucks up front. The rest to be awarded upon completion of the mission, should you choose to take it on."

I folded. I needed the money. I needed to get my tooth fixed. Pain chased ethics out the window. Or at least that was my official excuse, but, just between us, I have to admit that I was curious about Karin too. After all, new women don't show up in Blackhurst everyday and rumour had it that she was single....

* * *

The Report
Subject: Karin Mullerbeck   Age: 34
Orientation: Dyke   Sign: Libra
Tendencies: Vanilla

Introduction: It may be stated at the outset of this report, that the researcher found the subject to be a lively and interesting companion with a multi-faceted personality. Karin will be a dynamic addition to the community.

Materials and Methods: This study was conducted over a two week period in which the researcher spent a considerable amount of time with the subject. The period of study incorporates a women's weekend gathering, a three day canoe trip in a wilderness setting, and a domestic type, evening interaction. The report aims to examine various aspects of the subject's character and general demeanor in order to illuminate her significant strengths and weaknesses.

Literature Review: The researcher is now three-quarters of the way through *Lesbian Psychologies* and has read numerous novels and works on lesbian experience.

* * *

"What about lesbian sex? Surely you must have read something on lesbian sex?"

Tiiu. Always teasing. Trying to make me blush. I won't.

"What? You don't think lesbian sex is relevant to the report? It would be of interest. It would be of *great* interest, I assure you."

"What I really need is to be reading up on do-it-yourself dentistry. Can you believe that I can't get an appointment for two whole weeks? I'm going to die before then."

"Maybe Karin's a dentist? Why don't you find out."

One track minds...

* * *

Findings:

1. Women's Weekend Gathering
   a) First impressions

The researcher first became aware of the subject during a campfire sing-along involving approximately thirty women. It was dark when Karin arrived with some mutual acquaintances, but the researcher took note of the newcomer's striking appearance. The subject is tall and sturdy, well planted some might say, and has dark wavy hair that is feathered, shoulder length. She was dressed in baggy jeans and a deep pink sweatshirt. Part way through the event, researcher and subject were introduced. Her smile was warm. Her eyes are a rich brown. Although this interaction was brief, it left a positive initial impression.

   b) Political workshop

The researcher's next significant contact with the subject occurred the next day, at a workshop. As the workshop was of a political nature, the researcher took careful note of the subject's statements, attitudes and body language. Karin exhibited a significant understanding of and sensitivity to the issue at hand. She was not afraid to question the workshop leader or challenge other women in the room in a supportive yet astute manner. It was here that the researcher first took note of the subject's nervous habit of twirling her small hoop earring. This behaviour seemed to indicate tension or concentration in the subject. Her long fingers rolled the earring around and around, the gold hoop slipping effortlessly through the hole in her ear lobe. She caught me watching her. Smiled. She didn't look away. Held my gaze.

   c) Social interaction

Later that day, the researcher had an opportunity to dance with the subject. Karin's movements were fluid and graceful and she interacted pleasantly with her dance partner (the researcher). The volume of the music made conversation difficult and thus, the researcher and subject were unable to exchange anymore than a few casual words. At one point she asked the researcher "Is that the way you dance in Blackhurst?" Although the researcher initially took this remark to be judgmental, it later turned out it was not meant in that way. The subject explained that her judgment had been impaired, although not noticeably, and she was just trying to make small talk. It should be noted that the subject does not make excessive use of drugs, alcohol, or other mood altering substances. Also, Karin seems to maintain social decorum while under the occasional influence of such substances. More or less. At one point...

* * *

"Claire? Hi, it's me. The hired snoop."

"What's up kiddo?"

"I don't know about this report business. I like Karin. She's quite a neat woman."

"I hope you're going to be more descriptive than that in the report. Neat, eh?"

"Sometimes you guys amaze me. Can't you see anything strange about this? Doesn't it twig at your conscience at all? How would you like it if you showed up in some new place and got mushed onto a microscope slide for the vicarious viewing pleasure of the community? Maybe I should just give you guys your money back..." I didn't really mean it. I couldn't give the money back. My tooth, my tooth.

"Don't get wound up. You don't have to tell all. Just write something light-hearted, okay? It was meant mostly as a joke, but we want you to do it anyway. Besides, it's giving you the impetus to get to know a new *single* woman."

It was at that point that I began to suspect the motives of my friends.

* * *

3. Wilderness Setting

It is unclear to the researcher who initiated this phase of the study. During a phone conversation one week after the festival, either the subject or researcher suggested that they take advantage of their current flexibility (read: unemployment) and go canoeing. Together. Alone.

The subject proved to be a considerate, independent, yet helpful travel partner as well as an interesting person. This stage of the research enabled the researcher to have more significant contact with the subject. During the day, the researcher and subject paddled in companionable silence, speaking mostly only to note significant flora or fauna. Karin is knowledgeable about wildflowers and plants in particular. She undertook to teach the researcher plant anatomy. Petal, sepal. Anther, filament. Stigma, style, ovary. She is also a strong and well-seasoned outdoorswoman. When the researcher was in the stern, she observed the even and articulate paddling of the subject, muscles flexing to clear definition as she dipped and dipped her paddle into the shiny surface of the lake. The sun was hot. Her shoulders and neck were burnt pink around the edges of her white tank top.

Evenings provided the researcher the opportunity to have long conversations illuminating significant aspects of Karin's life history and experience. She has been out for nearly twelve years and has had a number of significant and insignificant lover relationships during this time. At the time of the trip she had been single and celibate for nearly eleven months. In that time, she has been working on redefining her relationship to herself and now feels open, once again, to sexuality with others. She said her main criteria for a lover is that she knows how to laugh. In bed, in particular. Her eyes glitter when she laughs. And she gets these little creases around the corners of her lips. Like dimples.

* * *

"Hi Laura. Do you have a moment to talk?"

"Depends. Is it business or pleasure?"

"Business, I guess." How ironic. I snort into the phone.

"Oh. *That* business. How's it going?"

"Ummmm... It's going."

"I hear you guys went on a canoe trip. That must've been useful for gathering information. Did you have a good time? I hope you didn't fall in."

"No. No one fell in. Laura... I... well..." What was it that I wanted to say? "Is there any way I can get out of this?"

"What? And keep us in the dark? Besides, we've paid you half the money already."

And I spent most of it. On supplies for the trip. Now I really needed the rest too.

"Oh shit! Got to go Laura. The cat is into the quiche. Call you back later." Saved. For now.

* * *

4. Domestic Situation

The subject and researcher returned from the four day canoe trip in good spirits and in need of baths. They went to the subject's house to unpack and separate their gear. The subject takes good care of her belongings. The subject's apartment is tidy without being obsessively so. It is tastefully decorated in late Sally Ann furniture, Latin American blankets and baskets, and lesbian-feminist memorabilia. (Including a wonderful mobile of naked purple ladies that rotates quietly in the steam rising from the claw-footed bathtub. Nice touch.) The subject sports an excellent collection of books covering a wide variety of issues, some of which were discussed during the wilderness phase of this study: Central American politics, feminist theory, lesbian erotica. The subject was open to loaning the researcher some books. She is an organized woman; she wrote down the titles of the borrowed books in a little purple notebook kept for that sole purpose.

The researcher and subject spent a quiet evening in her home, playing Scrabble and eating. Karin is a good Scrabble player. She also has a good appetite. She is a vegetarian and enjoys a wide variety of foods. She makes a mean curry and her apple crisp is yummy.

Her pancakes are delicious too.

* * *

Damn. I can't do this.

"Myla? Hi, it's me. The goddamn report writer."

"How's it going cutie? Haven't seen you in a while."

"Well, okay apart from my tooth. Actually wonderful. I guess."

"So. You finally got your bones jumped?"

"Myla!"

"Well?"

"I wish you wouldn't use that expression."

"So you did! Great! Bet it was nice. Karin's pretty sexy."

"Yes, it was nice, but in case you've forgotten, you guys are paying me a hundred dollars to do this. I really like this woman. What am I going to tell her? That my friends are paying me to sleep with her and then write about it? How slimy."

"There are worse things to do for a living. Besides, imagine how long it would have taken you to get into bed with her otherwise. Look what you can accomplish with a little incentive."

"I don't see making love with Karin as an accomplishment. Be serious pal. What am I going to do?"

"Write about it."

"Big help you are. Don't tell the others, eh?"

"Un-huh." Non-commital if I ever heard it. Shit.

* * *

Conclusion and Recommendations: The researcher finds that the subject, Karin Mullerbeck, is a friendly, warm, and dynamic person. She is well-rounded in her interests and open to new experiences and ideas. This researcher would recommend her to the Blackhurst Lesbian Community as an excellent addition to their circle, as a friend to some, lover to others.

* * *

Epilogue: That's all they get. But it won't stop them from prying for the details in person. Oh well. The details. What's there to say. We're spending time together. Eating. Hiking. Playing Scrabble. Dancing. Whatnot.

Eventually, I told her about the report. She laughed until her stomach hurt. Phew. Then she wanted to see it.

"What? I haven't written it."

"Why not?"

"Are you kidding Karin?"

"No. I'd love to read it. See how honest you are with yourself and your friends. I think it's very funny." More laughter. I like that about her.

"I can't believe you're not even a bit upset. I would flip if someone was hired to research me. And I'd go totally over the edge if that person ended up being my lover."

"So why'd you do it?"

Good question. I didn't tell her about my tooth. What was done, was done. I wrote the report and submitted it to the dreaded Seven. We were all back on Tiiu's porch two days later.

"Well, well," Tiiu welcomed me, "if it isn't the researcher who got overly involved with her subject."

"It blurs your objectivity, you know." Laura is such a smart ass.

"Maybe we should pay her only half in light of that." Piss off Sue. "Maybe we should make her pay *us* the $100."

"What for?"

"For motivating you to find a lover. You're much less bitchy when you're getting laid regularly." God, Laura bugs me.

"It seems to me that you did yourselves a favour. A deal's a deal. Pay up sisters. Pay up."

They did. Read it out loud first. Complained about the lack of juicy details. Laughed ourselves silly. I was glad it was over and done with. I went to the dentist the next day and got my toothache over and done with too. All clear on the Home Front.

Almost.

About a month later, Karin spotted a call for submissions to a collection of lesbian seduction stories. She asked me what I thought about submitting The Report.

"Me? I should think you're the one who might have something against that idea." She had eventually gotten around to being a bit pissed off, but not at me. We talked. We do a lot of that.

"Nah. It's written. It's silly. I'm for it. Just change my name. Women should have to do their own research."

"How's Karin Mullerbeck strike you as a pseudonym, my dear?"

"Good. Come kiss me."

And kiss we did.

The Tale of Bad Becky O.

WANDA WINFIELD

In 1842 a proper lady didn't travel alone by stagecoach, and I wouldn't have done so if circumstances had left me any other choice. I had just graduated from Miss Winston's School for Girls and was in my nineteenth year.

I was an orphan, my mother having died while nursing diphtheria patients two years earlier (among them Miss Winston's niece). Unlike my classmates, whose rich parents were busy planning opulent debutante balls and subsequent weddings, I was cast upon the world to make my own fortune.

A connection of Miss Winston's in the East knew of a situation for a governess to a well-to-do family. My options were somewhat limited, as teaching young ladies and governing children were the only occupations considered suitable for a gentlewoman of my reduced circumstances. Since having charge of two small children seemed preferable to teaching a class of perhaps a dozen giggling, spoilt ninnies, I decided to accept the post.

Now if a male relation had existed, I would have been escorted with proper supervision. Nonetheless, with only the example of my mother's spirit before me, I decided to make the journey alone, my head held high, not cowering in any corner.

The stagecoach on which I had booked my passage would have a tedious route indeed, I was told. Stops were scheduled in every town, to collect the state's revenue which was to be delivered to the capital at our journey's end. Extra guards rode on top of the coach, but passengers inside were scarce. A merchant of unpatented medicines and a banker were my travelling companions. Their conversation bored me, so as darkness began to fall, the rocking motion of the coach lulled me to a welcome sleep.

I don't know which sound it was that jolted me awake. It may have been the shouts of the men on top, or the crack of their rifles. Perhaps it was the hoofbeats approaching, ominously, like thunder.

The sudden braking of the coach threw me forward. I peered through the shaded window and saw a ring of horses around the coach, each masked rider carrying a torch and a pistol. The driver and guards, clearly out-numbered, were ordered down with their hands in the air.

Truly frightened, I began to remember stories of desperadoes and the outrages they would commit on any hapless female. My trembling fingers clutched at the hatpin Miss Winston had always told us to keep on or near our person, should our virtue need defending.

As the door was flung open, I felt the futility of this preparation with a sinking heart. In response to the silent gesture of the masked outlaw, I stepped out into the eerie torchlight.

One rider did not dismount and seemed to be in charge of the others, ordering them in low tones to remove the trunk containing the money. Slight of frame, yet moving with an agile grace, the outlaw seemed menacing, yet composed.

As I dared to raise my face, my eyes were met by the outlaw's, cool and grey beneath even brows. Suddenly, I knew who this was.

Even in the sheltered confines of Miss Winston's school, we had heard of Bad Becky O. Born Rebecca Overbrook, it was said that once she had led a peaceful life on her small dairy farm by the river, run with another woman, her lifelong companion, it seemed. Unconventional surely, but not enough to provoke censure.

Then came the railway builders who saw in this farm the perfect place for a crossroads. Money was offered, it was refused. The builders approached the state government. Suddenly, the women's title to the land was in question.

The railway men hired a posse to enforce the eviction order. Rebecca and Sarah met them in a wagon at the end of their lane with a shotgun held across Rebecca's lap, the reins to the team in Sarah's hands.

No one really knows what happened next. A gun went off and the team was startled, although it was later claimed that Rebecca started the horses deliberately. Another shot was fired, striking Sarah full in the chest. The hired posse scattered, leaving the fatally stricken woman in the arms of Rebecca.

When they returned later that night with the sheriff, the farmhouse was a smoking ruin; the livestock were all set free. In the months that followed, some said Rebecca had been seen running through the woods like a wild woman. It was rumoured she had died and it was only her ghost haunting the forest. Still other tales had her being taken in by those who saw her madness as a divine gift.

But there was no mystery at all to the report that she was seen in the mountains with a gang of desperate outlaws. Too many stories had her at their centre, plotting and carrying out the most daring robberies.

No private citizen lost their gold or valuables to her gang. Only the state treasury was depleted, as each time a payroll was delivered or revenue collected, the trunk was spirited away before it reached its destination. The money she had scorned before, she now claimed as her due.

This was the notorious woman who now stood before me.

"Oh please," I cried, flinging myself on my knees before her. "Have mercy on a poor, orphaned maiden. By your countenance I can see you are no ruffian. Please defend the honour of a gentlewoman!"

Against the raucous laughter of the other outlaws, I heard two words addressed to me in a level tone: "Get up." With a motion of the rifle barrel, I was gestured back into the coach.

I scrambled in, glad to be away from the leering eyes of the gang. Surely now I would be safe, I thought. As the coach lurched into motion, I tried to imagine where my rescuer was taking me. I was surprised, therefore, when we stopped again so soon.

I heard the crunch of boots on the road and saw my liberator standing in the coach doorway, cast in shadow by the bright moonlight. With the same lithe movement I had seen before, the robber swung into the coach and occupied the seat across from me.

"You know who I am." It was a statement, not a question.

Mesmerized I nodded, then sensing a verbal reply was expected, I took a deep breath and said in a rush, "You're Miss Rebecca Overbrook." I was jarred by the harsh laugh that greeted this remark. Had I been wrong? But no, for as the mask was finally lowered, I could see the full, strong mouth of a woman and her smooth yet defiant jaw.

"Honey, no one's called me that since you were in pantaloons playing hopscotch."

I blushed at this reference to my undergarments and felt unsettled by the peculiar sentiment that somehow this woman had the ability to see right through me. Nettled by her reference to my youth, I shot back, "All right. You're Bad Becky O."

A hoot of laughter followed, but this time I did not feel it was aimed at me derisively. She grinned at me and I could sense some admiration. Encouraged, I smiled back.

"And who might you be, on the road at this late hour?" she asked.

"My name's Emily Harper and I'm going East to be a governess." As soon as I said it, I bit my lip, thinking that she would laugh at me, but she didn't. Leaning back and regarding me gravely, she said, "Well, Miss Emily, what am I going to do with you?"

I thought about her setting me free, and her riding off with her gang. I would never see her again. I would go teach Latin to the children of my employers while she would ride free through the mountains by moonlight, chestnut hair flowing behind her like a centaur's tail. Something clutched at my heart. I wanted to remain with her at least till morning. It must have showed in my eyes because she said, "I'm going to take you back to my hideout. You'll be safe there tonight."

As easily as quicksilver, she swung out of the coach and onto the driver's seat. I heard the crack of the whip and felt the horses plunge into their traces. Some time later we stopped and I was let out into the inky night. A blindfold was unnecessary. So total was the darkness that I could not have identified our location. I heard the creaking of a rough wooden door and nearly tripped as I stumbled through it.

I stood there shivering in the damp chilliness. As the flame in the coal lamp grew, I saw enough of my surroundings to surmise that I was in a bare mountain shack.

"Not much of a home, but I did build it myself," she said cheerily.

"Really?" I was astonished. She seemed to enjoy my surprise.

"Honey, you don't know half my talents," she said chuckling, then seriously, "A woman can be whatever she wants."

I nodded slowly, gravely. Here at last was what I had hungered for without knowing it. A kindred spirit with whom to share that simple truth. She smiled at me.

"Why don't you get your things off while I get this wood stove started? Here's some blankets to wrap yourself in. There's only one bed, but it's big enough for two. You're not afraid to sleep with me, are you?" I shook my head and she replied, "Good. Then maybe you can let go of that damned hatpin you've been clutching."

I blushed, and to cover my confusion I busied myself in removing layers of outer clothing and petticoats, followed by my stockings and corset. Shivering in only my thin bodice and cotton drawers, I got under the bulky, woollen blankets and thick quilt. I wondered fleetingly if Sarah had made the quilt as Becky did not seem capable of such fine, painstaking work. Again, she read my mind.

"I like to keep that near me. It reminds me of Sarah."

The stove now glowed with warmth and by its light I watched Becky undress. In a girls' boarding school I must have watched dozens of girls prepare for bed, but none affected me the way she did. I could not stop staring at her broad shoulders, her firm breasts, and flat belly.

"I don't bother with fussy nightclothes," she said casually, as she removed the last of her clothing and eased her naked body in beside mine. The surge of unfamiliar emotions made me feel quite dizzy. I shivered and she raised herself on one elbow and asked me, "Are you cold?"

"No—yes," I stammered, trying to hide my conflicting feelings. She put her arm around me and drew me close. Hesitantly, I put my arm around her. We lay quite still, our bodies touching but not moving as she slowly stroked my back.

"Better?" she whispered.

"Oh yes," I whispered back, not daring to trust my voice. I could feel her breasts pressing against mine through my bodice.

"Did you ever sleep with a woman before?" she asked.

"Oh yes," I replied. "Lots of times in my boarding school, when it was cold, Miss Winston told us to double up in our beds."

"And was there a particular friend you liked to share with?" she asked.

Memories of Pamela flooded my mind. "An older girl liked me best, I think. We would lie together like this, holding each other so tight we could hardly breathe, and then we would just lie still and listen to each other's breathing and heartbeats, and long so much for ... I don't know what."

Becky chuckled in the darkness. "For love, darling, that's what. Haven't you ever woken up from a delicious dream of love, feeling as warm and moist as if it's just taken place? Did you think that only men and women could enjoy the fruits of love?"

She took my hand and kissed my fingers gently, then ran the tip of her tongue down each one into the palm of my hand. She then placed her own fingers gently on my lips. I kissed them and sucked each one. She put her fingers on her own lips while I continued to lick them. She lowered her face to mine till I could feel her breath. Then through her own fingers, I felt her tongue touch mine. Gently she withdrew her hand and explored my mouth with her tongue.

My own took on a life of its own and soon they were writhing and twisting together. Her hand travelled down to my bosom. I moaned softly as she deftly opened the buttons of my bodice. My nipple sprang to life in her palm. Swiftly she freed my other breast from its flimsy covering. Her fingers worked their way lightly in circles to the centre of my breasts. Panting now, my bosom swelled up to meet her.

Her lips brushed my cheek, my ear, and then travelled downward along my neck until they reached my nipples. First one, and then the other, she slowly sucked and rolled about in her mouth, with her tongue tracing circles around them.

I was nearly wild with excitement. Now her other hand trailed down my belly, across my hip and came to rest on the fleshy mound covered in luxuriant, curly black hair. I could feel dampness seeping through. Her fingers easily slid up through the loose drawers to rest directly upon my hair. Gently probing with her finger, she found the creamy centre and followed it upward to the very tip where I thought I would scream if she lingered. Instead she returned below and stroked gently upward, again and again, while the tension mounted in my groin and belly.

Then just as I thought I could stand it no more, she slid herself down until her mouth was over me. Pulling off my drawers, she parted my legs and applied her tongue to my innermost recesses. Quickly I was brought to a supreme concentration of intense delight, which exploded in waves, sending cascades of blinding light through my nerves, out from the centre of my body to its furthest extremes. I screamed and writhed in ecstatic abandon. After a while the waves subsided and I lay exhausted and content.

"Now you know what love is darling," she whispered in my ear. I turned to her and held her tight. Soon we began our dance of delight again, our bodies moving in time to the rhythm they could sense. With my awakened senses, my body followed its natural impulses and soon I was kneeling between her thighs lapping the juice from that fruit for which I had so longed, but not known existed.

Eventually we had feasted to our hearts' fullness on each other, and fell asleep, cradled by the night and bathed in the shimmer of starlight.

In the morning I begged her to let me stay.

"It's no life," she said, "for a pure and gentle soul like yours. Go to your new position, learn the dignity of honest labour, and don't ever, ever let anyone tell you you're only a woman. For now you know what a fine and precious creation that is. As for me, I have learned that love can live again in me. Perhaps the debts of the past have been paid and it is time to go on living."

Weeping, I left her and stumbled over the rocks on my way down to the road where the next coach would find me. I told the passengers I had been set free during the night and had found my way home. No one has ever known how true that is.

Zoe

N. HOLTZ

Zoe was my least successful lesbian love affair. She had the darkest eyes I'd ever seen on a white person and a fucked up combination of shaved and long, unnaturally black hair. She had a tall, lean body which she abused with coke when she could afford it.

When I first met her she said she was into men, but I knew what she *was* (or soon would be). Men feared her and she liked that. She enjoyed dominating young skinhead boys — only for a while — then she'd get bored. There was the intense way she reached out and demanded my attention, with her fabulous, elegant nostrils flaring as she said, "You're full of shit."

Zoe spent two months ignoring me, making fun of me, and following me around. I'd run into her at certain trendy loft parties and at the Labrinth, an industrial-disco bar that catered to all sexual types but mostly exhibitionists. Zoe would stand at the edge of the dance floor checking out the dykes. But if a woman came over with a second drink in hand, she'd instantly huddle up to her gay male friends. She let me get closer, maybe because I'd been known to fuck boys or maybe just because we liked the same kind of loud, raunchy music not too many girls are into. One night, at the Labrinth, bored of her usual games, I started to get dressed to leave.

"You're going?" she asked, alarmed. Her eyes were furious.

"I don't feel like waiting until midnight for you to pay some attention to me," I replied sulkily, pulling a bulky, black sweater over my head. She reached over and jerked the sweater down into my Levis, her fingers quickly brushing my bare navel and then my pubic hair. Just as quickly, she disappeared.

At home, in my room, I paced. Her body is warm, sure, like a lizard's eye, I scribbled into my journal with scarlet nail polish. I blew one of my speaker's playing the Violent Femmes, "Why can't I get just one screw, why can't I get close to you,..."

Impatient and bored with the sexual tension, the next time I saw her, I asked her whether or not she fucked girls.

"You mean, am I into you?" she replied smugly.

"Yes," I hissed.

"What do you think?" was her non-answer. I decided she got off on having power over me because I wanted her. She didn't really like me, so I thought, fuck it.

A few days later, I came home after a crummy day at work and my roommate told me a woman had been waiting for me in my room but had left suddenly. My room is filled with silk cloth and rugs. A futon takes up a large part of it, and the floor is cluttered with pillows, records, and candles. On the wall hang posters of female punk and metal bands, nude pictures of my favorite porn stars, black lace bras, bodices, and a pair of handcuffs. The room is supposed to operate as a Venus Fly Trap capturing the sexier occupants, but Zoe had twice escaped it. This time, though, she left traces. Her black fishnet tights lay draped over my speaker and my open journal was on my bed. I blew a second speaker playing Marianne Faithful's "Why'd Ya Do It."

The next day I sent her a fortune cookie with a message inside: cunnilingus doesn't suck.

The following night when I came home, my roommate had taped a message to my door: "The back door lock was picked but nothing seems to be missing." When I stripped and crawled into my futon, I figured out who the criminal was by the lingering smell of her Camel cigarettes and Coco Chanel perfume. I found an empty bottle of her perfume on the floor and put it in me, coming in a long, tight string of orgasms.

Her games were making me crazy; I tried to forget about her. To this end, I spent long hours after work in trendy cafes, twisting my dreadlocks, listening to Kashtin, and eating cheesecake. Except I kept having these fantasies of the two of us getting busted for possession and sent to jail. I conjured up images of her naked, her warm nipples pressed against the cool, metal bars of the cell and me behind her, my tongue and teeth buried in her firm ass, my fingers deep in her tight cunt while a female screw with a military haircut watched.

One evening, a strange woman with long, sleek red hair and a white jumpsuit strode into the bistro and up to my table. She murmured a few incomprehensible phrases in German and tossed me a gold lipstick: Currant Stain by Yves St. Laurent. I rolled it open and discovered a tightly folded piece of paper. It said, *Je veux te baiser, Z.* I smiled slowly and crossed my legs. My clit swelled with anticipation.

Two nights later, Zoe lay on my futon, her hand twisting through my pet cat's fur, making me wet with wanting them inside me. I took my cat from her hands and tossed it out the door.

"Why'd you do that?" she asked lazily. I came over and sat on the edge of the futon, next to her.

"I got your message from the German girl," I said.

"Actually, she's a he. You're the only girl I hang out with," she said, gazing intently at her fingernails with their chipped black nail polish. Finally, she sighed and added, "I only sorta did this once and that was like a long time ago."

"Do you want to forget about it?" I asked, trying not to sound whiney or pissed off. For an answer, she edged closer to me. She picked up my hand and it chilled me.

"It's no coincidence my hand is cold," she warned me. I ignored this and slipped my hand through a hole in her jeans. I explored the inside of her thighs, my hand straining against the tight material.

"I first wanted to fuck you when we ran into each other at the rep cinema. You sat beside me in a really ripped pair of jeans and your legs were apart and you said, 'Hey chick, how was your weekend?'"

"How seductive you are," she said, smiling sarcastically. Then she kissed me ferociously, her tongue all over my mouth, teeth, and gums. I sucked her tongue. She bit my lower lip, hard, and pulled away. I gave her a very hostile look and crossed the room to get a drink.

I was pouring straight scotch down my throat when she came up behind me, took my drink away, dug her nails into my shoulders and bit my neck. I stood still and pretended to ignore her and she laughed at me. She ran a finger across one of my nipples, making it hard then along my bare arms, making them shiver. She pulled my t-shirt off and slipped the straps of my black velvet bra off my shoulders. She pushed her hand across my flat, bare stomach, down into my jean shorts, over my underwear. She pulled my underwear tightly over my clit and started rubbing. Within minutes my cunt started contracting and I thought, if she doesn't stop, I'm going to come soon. I wiggled around, put my hands on the side of her face and kissed her slowly with lots of tongue. Then I leaned down and licked her nipples through the white cloth of her Lunachicks t-shirt, making wet stains. I pulled her jeans down and brought my head towards her cunt, but before I started I pulled away and said,

"If you wanna stop now..."

"You must be kidding," she answered and pushed me into a 69 position, not something I usually go for. She shoved my jean shorts down and started eating me in a very sloppy but thorough way, sometimes biting my pubic hair hard, sending little jolts of pain and pleasure through my system. In return, I slapped her ass and hungrily licked her clit. She kept bringing me to the brink of orgasm, over and over. I pinched her and panted, "C'mon bitch, let me come."

She smiled sleazily, "Uh, uh, me first."

We shifted position, facing each other, started necking again, pushing our small, hard nipples together, grinding our clits and pubic bones. This soon became monotonous, so I jammed my kneecap into her pussy. She moaned and said, "Fuck me." I scanned my room and spotted a slim, plastic Body Shop bottle of vanilla skin cream. I opened it, smeared some on her cunt, then started to pump her with it. Licking her clit hard, and reaching up to twist her nipples every now and then, I brought her to the point of no return. "I want this, I want this," she repeated like a mantra, her face screwed up as she pulled my hair. I was gratified to see her, all animal and convulsing cunt. But I wasn't happy to see her crash out.

"What about me?" I asked, bumping my clit against her thigh.

"Do it yourself," she murmured through half-closed lids.

"Fine," I said and began pushing a couple of my fingers into the edge of my slippery, wet, needy pussy, filling with a sweet ache. As I started to come, she pulled my fingers out and began to play with my clit and soon my body was all rhythym, friction and tease. I came, yelling her name, rings of pleasure twisting free from my cunt. She touched my damp cheeks, her mouth surprised, her head nestled under my armpit. I slid my hand down along her backbone and across her ass. Before long we started again. It didn't end until four or five a.m. or whenever her restless body woke me. She told me she was going to the can when really she was leaving me.

Brown Cows and VapoRub

CAROLYN GAMMON

A salt-stained boot kicked the door shut; Bea's hands were full.

"I think I've got it all." She pulled items from a Jean Coutu plastic bag, like Mary Poppins. "Vicks VapoRub, Halls Mentholyptus, cherry-flavoured, a tisane just for throats — lemme read you the ingredients: peppermint leaf, ginger root, coltsfoot leaf, yum, yum..."

"Kleenex..." Her cold care litany was interrupted by a feeble call.

"Yes, got the Kleenex, dyke-sized."

"I mean, han' me some pwease." The clogged voice came from a pile of pillows, an out-stretched hand. Bea dropped the tissue and rushed to Ana. "You poor darling," she took off her scarf and wrapped it around Ana's neck, "you look *miserable*."

"I need Kleenex, not flattery," Ana said, making a move toward the box.

"Don't move, I'll get it."

The next moments were taken up with much honking and snuffling.

Bea was in the kitchen making throat tea when Ana's slightly less nasal voice piped up from the bedroom. "Thanks for coming over Bea. I don't think I could even crawl to a *dépanneur*."

"You shouldn't be going out. It's like minus twenty out there and icy." Bea swept sideways through the door with a tray, a dishtowel spread over her forearm in mock civility. "Tea is served, madame." She set a steaming mug in front of Ana.

"This is the sixth day. I can't believe it, this fucking *grippe* just doesn't let up." Ana sipped the tea. "One moment, I'm chatting on the phone, the next moment, *gag*, a mucous monster clutches my throat, I throw down the phone..."

"Speaking of which," Bea broke in, "have you heard from Candy?"

"Yeah, she called last night, having a *great* time, the film fest is *great*, she saw a play ... whiiiineee! Why isn't she here to Florence Nightingale me?"

Bea looked slightly annoyed. "No, no," Ana took her hand. "You are definitely a superb stand-in, but Candy has this patented cuddling remedy."

"You mean fuck remedy."

"Well, that too," Ana sighed.

Ana's tea was finished and Bea was looking through tapes.

"So I thought of an entertainment ploy for this cozy winter afternoon."

"You're going to play me Cris Williamson, Holly Near, and Meg Christian until I'm cooed back to health. 'Sweet womaaam, risin' so fineee.'"

"No-o..."

"Wait, I've got it, you'll play me Melissa Etheridge ... or Carol Pope! and I'll be slutted into health. 'She's a cool blond, steaming bitch, she makes my body twitch,...'"

"Closer! I thought we could tell each other stories." Bea cued a Mercedes Sosa tape. "Seduction stories."

"Sounds more fun than blowing my nose!" Ana said, reaching for another Kleenex. "But first, would you please dump these for me?"

A pile of used tissues had gathered by the bed. Bea brought her the garbage.

"I've got an added feature though," Ana said, playing basketball with the Kleenex wads. "We have to name categories for one another, like hottest, most romantic … most plugged up."

"Are you sure you're in the mood?"

"Yes … yes, joke. So, do they have to be true?"

"They have to *sound* true," Bea answered.

Bea set herself up with another pile of pillows at the far end of the bed, her toes contacting Ana's under the comforter.

"You first," Ana said. "I'm sick and need longer to think."

"What category?"

"Hmmmm," Ana wrinkled her forehead in consideration. "Most romantic is too soppy. How about most … bizarre?"

Bea sat back and thought for a while. Seeing Ana shiver, she retrieved a shawl and upped the thermostat. The sun was setting and a golden glow took over the room as she began.

"Once upon a time, in my pre-historic het days, I was invited to this party in Dorval…"

"The 'burbs! A suburban myth! That's even better!"

"I was invited by this lesbian friend. I mean, I knew she was lesbian, but somehow I was surprised to find only women there — I'd never been to a party without men."

"How old were you?"

"Eighteen. I'd just moved out on my own. Anyway, I was definitely nervous and drank too much, too fast. At first I clung to Gerry, but as the evening wore on she disappeared into a corner smooching with this woman in a pantsuit, leaving me to fend for myself. I was sitting on this couch…"

"Vinyl, right?"

"I don't know…"

"You remembered the pantsuit."

"I was sitting on this couch with my Brown Cow…"

"You drank Brown Cows?"

"I was eighteen. Look, give your larynx a break and lemme tell my story!"

"Sorry," Ana stuck a pillow in her mouth as evidence of a vow of silence.

"So I'm nursing this Brown Cow when this woman came up to me..."

"The plot thickens."

Bea glared at Ana before continuing. "She was dressed in black leather, I mean *all* leather: pants, jacket, and one of those caps the boys in the Village wear, and cowgirl boots with metal toes."

"And you hadn't noticed her before?"

"Well yeah, but I never imagined she'd come up to me. So she asks me to dance! When I stood, I musta been half a foot taller than her. I'm looking down at the top of her cap wondering what the fuck I'm doing in Dorval with Ms. Petite Leather, when she pulls me in closer for a slow and I'm suddenly getting into it. The party's getting smaller and Ms. Leather is asking me for one dance after the other and some of the remaining women start to take their shirts off."

"Oooo-weee! Mini-Michigan in Dorval!"

"And I find myself in the with the rowdies..."

"Or the SMers."

"Hey now, don't make assumptions. This is my story. So the leather woman..."

"What was her name anyway?"

"Constance. She unzipped her jacket and undid the buttons on her shirt during a break between songs. Then she looked at me, or my chest as if to say, it's your turn. Now I was kind of stuck 'cause I had a turtleneck on..."

"A woman who takes chances! Whaddya do?"

"I thought, what the hell, and I peeled it off."

"Atta dyke!" Ana cheered.

"I had a bra on and besides, I was *not* a dyke yet."

"Details, details."

"Needless to say, the slows were getting hotter and hotter..."

"I'm getting too hot," Ana broke in. "I mean the temperature in here, it's these bloody chill and heat waves."

Bea got up to turn down the thermostat and put on a Ma Rainey tune: 'Went out last night with a crowd of my friends, they musta been womens 'cause I don't like no mens.' She grabbed Ana's jean jacket off the nearby chair to demonstrate a slow. "She'd lean into me like this and my tits came to her chin level."

"I have yet to see what's so bizarre about this, sounds like a pretty normal suburban seduction to me," Ana yawned.

"Wait, I'm getting there. Finally Ms. Leather reaches around my neck — I thought she was going to kiss me — and she says 'C'mon babe, let's go to the other room.' She called me 'babe'! She just assumed I was lesbian; I thought I was pretty obviously straight."

"What did you look like at the time?"

"Long hair, earrings, lipstick, the whole bit."

"She thought you were fem, and you were at a lesbian party after all. How was she supposed to know?"

"How was I supposed to know? I thought a party for women was like a hen party, I guess. Anyway, when she said that, I think I had what you might call one of those crisis moments in a het woman's life. I thought, now or never..."

"And you chose now?"

"Are you kidding? I didn't say a word. I pretended I hadn't heard a thing and when the music ended I disentangled myself as quickly as possible." Bea tossed the jean jacket over the chair to illustrate her point.

Ana booed from her end of the bed, "I want my money back!"

"I was desperate, the Brown Cows were wearing off, and I just wanted to find Gerry and get out of there. I was looking all over and finally saw her shoes sticking out of the hall closet."

"She was getting it on?"

"If only. I'd have yanked her out, clits sizzling or not, and made her drive me home. No, she was out of it, drunk, blotto. It was three a.m., Metro closed and much too expensive for a taxi."

"The plot re-thickens."

Ana was sinking lower into the pillows, her eyelids puffed and heavy.

"Look, before you go on, there's this tiny porcupine stuffed up my nose and my head feels like a pin cushion. Sorry."

Bea got up immediately and went back to her shopping bag.

"You need a Vicks inhalation."

"I thought those went out with mustard plasters."

Ignoring the scepticism, Bea put on the kettle. The phone rang.

"It's Candy," Bea sang, handing the receiver to Ana.

"Hi!... Yes, still sick. How's T.O? ... Yeah, she's over here babying me to death, I mean to health.... Oh, you know, asparagus tips, Cuban rum, Vicks inhalations.... I don't know, I'm about to find out.... Okay, you too, love you... bye."

Ana straggled out of bed into the dining room.

"This is the longest trip I've made in days," Ana joked. She looked askance at the bowl of steaming water with oil slicks of Vicks VapoRub.

"Just get under that towel and breathhhhhe." Ana stuck her head under. Bea stood behind and started massaging her shoulders.

"If I'd known a back rub came with it, I'd have jumped at it!"

"Shut-up and breathe."

"How long do I have to stay here?"

"Till your nostrils clear."

"Till next week you mean."

"Try five minutes at least." Bea continued massaging to keep her patient happy. Ana popped her face out from the towel.

"So continue, I need to be entertained." Bea jerked the towel back over her face.

"Quiet and breathe or I won't." Noting compliance, Bea continued.

"Where were we? Oh yes, my chum was out for the night in the closet, Ms. Leather had wandered off to the chip bowl, and it was three a.m. I didn't know what to do. I guess Constance saw I was in distress 'cause she came my way again. I just froze. All the sweat from the dancing had congealed on me and I was tired. I noticed she'd done her shirt and jacket back up and I figured, oh, she's leaving. And I was disappointed. Like when it was a possibility I was scared, but the moment the chance was gone, I wanted it. Do you know what I mean?"

"Yeah, it happened to me once in P-town," Ana's voice came towel-muffled. "I was waitressing and this Australian chick kept coming by and leaving really big tips. I ignored her for days and then she came in with her girlfriend."

"It's not quite the same."

"Well, I was disappointed."

"So nothing happened?"

"Actually, she'd brought her girlfriend in to show me off; they wanted a threesome."

"Did you go for it?"

"You have to wait till it's my turn ... I think five minutes are up. My face feels like a prune." Ana leaned her head back from the bowl, into Bea's massaging hands; her face was blotchy and wet. Bea towelled Ana's face off gently. Ana pressed one nostril with her forefinger and tried to breathe; it was blocked. She tried the other and a breath went in.

"Victory!" she yelled, jumping to her feet, and planting a hot-lipped Vicks kiss on Bea's cheek.

"What did I tell you? My grandmother used to make us kids do that, worked every time, then she'd give us gingersnaps."

"Mmmm, wish we had some. How about some cocoa?"

"Hot lemonade for you!" Bea replied and headed back to the kitchen.

Resettled in the bedroom, Bea put on some Danielle Messia. The singer's low, swelling voice filled the room where the sun had once been. Ana lit a candle.

"*Enfin*, the seduction scene!" Bea announced, cozying up on a second pile of pillows next to Ana.

"Hold it, let's re-cap. Last we know, Ms. Leather was on her way out the door."

"No, I said I *thought* she was 'cause she'd done her jacket back up."

"Are you sure this story doesn't fall into the 'most protracted' category?" Ignoring Ana, Bea continued.

"So Constance says to me, 'Ton amie est partie?' I said yes, in a manner of speaking, and I couldn't afford a taxi and whatnot. And d'you know what she did?"

"Ripped your clothes off and had an orgy with you and the rest of the gals?"

"She offered to pay my cab fare home. Wasn't that nice?"

"This is your story? I can't believe I've waited through a Vicks inhalation and hot lemonade for this."

"You are *sooo* patient. No, it's not over yet, you have more suffering to come."

"I'll need another massage."

"Okay, so I'll speed up. Essentially, I'd started to see the absurdity in the situation and Constance seemed nice enough, so I said no, maybe I'd just hang around till the Metro opened at six. She offered to make me another Brown Cow, but I'd had it with drinks, so I just sat on the couch and had some chips. Constance sat beside me and we started chatting. She worked for Xerox, an office job. I guess I was surprised. I supposed she worked on construction or something."

"Stereotypes," Ana shook her finger.

"And she apologized for coming onto me on the dance floor! I said no problem and we sat there in silence for a while." Bea remained silent, then took Ana's hand and began caressing it.

"You did that?"

"Yeah, I don't know why. Only it was like being on a date with a boyfriend and it seemed the natural thing to do."

"What did Constance do?"

"She smiled."

"That's it?"

"No ... then I did this," Bea said, running her hand through the hair on the side of Ana's head. "And she did this," Bea placed a hand on Ana's thigh.

"Hold it, I'll be Constance and you be you," Ana suggested, placing her hand on Bea's thigh.

"What next?" Ana asked.

"She just put her hand there, and you know, I'd been in that situation with a man and really resented it, but this time I just felt good."

"How long did you sit there feeling good?"

"Awhile."

"Hot, really hot."

"Then I put my hand on her hand," Bea put her hand over Ana's. "And I moved her hand along my thigh to my crotch."

"Ooouuu, the good old groin approach," Ana said, patting Bea's inner thigh affectionately.

"Then she put her other hand over my hand," Ana responded by placing her other hand, now stacked three high. Bea continued with the narrative.

"And she stopped me moving her hand and asked if I really wanted that. Guess what I did?"

"Really, I can't guess anymore."

"I hauled off and kissed her."

"On the hand?"

"On the lips, you jerk."

"Excuse me, you just seemed to be into hands."

"Speaking of which," Bea said, "your hands are really cold. Are you warm enough?"

"Actually, I could use that shawl again and where are my cough drops?"

Bea broke from their cozy position to hunt down the cough drops. "More throat tea," she announced.

"You're joking. I'm going to float away if I have one more thing to drink."

"Then float. I'm making tea and supper too. What's in your fridge?"

"Use anything that's not furry," Ana replied. "I think I'll rest a bit. But what happened anyway?"

"I'll tell you at supper. I don't think you're up to hearing about a hot sex scene."

"What! Tell me, tell me."

"Forget it. Rest, eat, and then I'll tell."

"You're so..."

"Rest." Bea blew out the candle and disappeared into the kitchen.

She let Ana sleep for a couple of hours and had hot noodles with ricotta cheese ready when Ana woke up coughing.

"Poor baby, drink this." She held out a mug of the promised throat tea.

"My bladder's bursting, bathroom first."

They supped, listening to a call-in radio show. The question of the evening was: should Canada join Free Trade with Mexico? Ana and Bea made snide remarks during most of the calls.

"They should work first on getting a free trade of lesbians across the U.S. border!" Bea suggested, pretending to reach for the phone.

Ana started getting riled. "Why do they have these programs anyway? Free airtime for racists? Call 514-BIGOT," she chanted in an operator's voice. Bea clicked off the radio.

"Ana darling, it's not good to get wrought-up when you're sick."

"Sick? Just *who* is sick in this society?"

"Ana, noodles." Bea speared some of the remaining supper and offered it to Ana.

"Mothers!" Ana scowled, then smiled at Bea. "This pasta is going down my poor throat really nice. You know, I really appreciate you being here." Ana reached for Bea's hand across the table. They intertwined fingers.

"I know," Bea said.

Supper was over and Bea had ordered her patient back into her mound of pillows.

"I didn't mean to cut you off. We can talk about Free Trade if you want to," Bea offered in a lacklustre tone.

"No, that's all right. It's just when I'm sick I lie here all day, listening to the radio, reading the newspapers — you're the first human I've had to rant at in a bit."

"I told you, ranting is not on your cold care list of activities."

"Okay, so you weren't finished that story, were you?"

"You want to hear the rest?"

"Of course! Weren't we at the three-hand stack?" Ana asked, re-stacking their hands.

"No, we'd made it to me laying a kiss on Constance," Bea corrected.

"Right. So you were necking."

"Right. So then after a bit, Constance says maybe we should go into the other room. By this time I was creaming my jeans. Actually, I think I was wearing cords. She said she'd tuck me in."

"That is so *sweet!*"

"Yeah, she was a really sweet woman. She took my hand and led me to the room. I'll never forget it. There was a bowl of Avon heart-shaped soaps on the dresser, doilies everywhere, and there was one of those black velvet and sparkles paintings of..."

"The Virgin Mary."

"Are you joking? Dolly Parton!"

"Dolly's a dyke?"

"Don't you read the tabloids?"

"But that was years ago."

"Dolly's *been* a dyke for years, though I didn't know that then. I just thought Constance had a thing for country and western singers, and in the painting Dolly had boots just like Constance!"

"So what happened?"

"Well, again, she offered to tuck me in and leave, but I was saying no, please stay and it was a bit awkward because she knew that it would be my first time. I was so hot though, I swear if she'd just breathed on my crotch I'd have come."

"Did she?"

"She helped me off with my turtleneck and I undid her jacket and blouse, though she didn't want to take them off. Then when I went to unsnap her leather pants she stopped me. Instead she took my pants off slowly, so I was sitting there just in my underwear. Then she undid her own pants and this thing spronged out at me!"

"What?"

"She was packing a dildo!"

"The entire night?"

"Sure."

"And you didn't notice?"

"Her pants were thick, and frankly, I wasn't looking for it."

"What did it look like?"

"It was really good quality, leather..."

"What else?"

"Brown leather and a black leather harness."

"Did you freak out?"

"Actually no, I figured, hey, I know what this is all about. I was almost relieved..."

"So then you fucked."

"Well..."

"Don't tell me after all this you didn't get it on? You, the dildo queen?"

"That's a recent reputation. Remember, I was eighteen, straight, or so I thought, it was four or five a.m., after four or five Brown Cows, strange house..."

"Dolly Parton in velvet and sparkles..."

"Yeah, all that. We started to ... but I was just overwhelmed and..."

"You started to cry."

"You guessed it." Bea and Ana both laughed, as if such a scenario were common to both. Ana cuddled up to Bea and put an arm about her shoulder.

"Still, that's a pretty, damn good story. What did Constance do?"

"She was so nice, just like before, really gentle. She asked why I was crying and I couldn't really say. I remember she kept saying 'Ça va, ma cherie,' over and over, kept calling me 'ma cherie.' And I kept saying really, it's all right. We ended up cuddling and sleeping. I remember when we woke the next day she wasn't wearing the dildo."

"Or the leather jacket."

"Not either," Bea laughed. "And she looked really different without her clothes on, even smaller. I'd not thought about her age the night before, but in the morning I saw these wrinkles in her face and she must have been in her mid-thirties, which was old for me then. She was still sleeping and my arms went right around her and I felt like the stronger one. I thought of her at the office and wondered if she felt out of place..."

"Or if she packed the dildo there too!"

"You are incurable!" Bea slapped Ana's arm away from where it had been resting on her shoulder.

"Well, that story's not so bizarre," Ana said.

"I guess not. I think I just wanted to tell it."

"That was your first lesbian experience?"

"Yes, but unfortunately, it took me six more years to come out. The night had been weird enough that I filed it under 'experiments' and went on fucking men. But when I did come out I think that one night with Constance helped me 'cause I came out really fast and didn't have all these hesitations that I hear some dykes talk about. I knew it could be sweet with a woman."

The two sat in silence. It was late and Bea was looking at her watch. After a while Ana spoke.

"I don't suppose I have to tell a story now."

"If you want. What about the threesome in P-town? You can do a threesome category, but it'll have to be a time-lapse version. The Metros close in half an hour."

"Okay, I got one and I'll make it short. But I'd rather tell a recent one..."

"Oh yeah?"

"Yeah," said Ana, hesitating before she spoke. "Like tonight. I really liked it when you massaged me and I liked it when we were doing the three-hands on thigh thing, and ... just sitting close."

"Are you coming on to me?"

"I'm saying I liked all that. Did you?"

"Yes," Bea said reflectively.

They sat for a while in silence. Ana took Bea's hand.

"You could stay the night you know," Ana offered.

"I don't have the stuff for my contacts," Bea answered.

"And I'm pretty sick still," Ana reasoned.

"Maybe another time?"

"Yeah, I'd really like that."

Bea made sure that there was a box of Kleenex by the side of Ana's bed, cough drops within reach, and the comforter well tucked in. She went into the bedroom with her jacket on to say goodnight.

"Gimme a kiss," Ana said.

"I'll get your cold," Bea countered.

"Then I can come take care of you."

"That's true," Bea said, leaning over the bed.

Woman In Colour

CAROL CAMPER

When I dream of you, I dream in colour.
Yellow.
Because of my August birthday, I am the Lioness.
Yellow on yellow savannah.
Hunger compels me to stalk you.
Yellow grasses
at first obscure my presence
as I wait and watch:
inside me an absence and dire longing.
You know I am here.
It is only a matter of time before the question is answered.
Will you be mine today
or some other's?
Will you be mine another day?
Eyelids lower as my focus intensifies
on you.
My whole body tightens and trembles
as if I were really going to resist
the coiled-spring explosion that will hurl me toward you.
One split-second now,
as the yellow, heavy, equatorial sun burns
this image into the lioness mind that watches you.

And now I have come for you,
mesmerized by beauty,
wanting you the only way I can truly have you
— all.
The leaping path, the crazy zigzags
this day all lead to me.
When I make love to your beautiful mouth, my darling
I feast.
There seems to be infinite variety in our sensuality.
Other delights set aside for now,
we take our time as we take our pleasure.
Sweet honeywine from your reddened lips
makes me drunk with pleasure, my love.
Silky plumpness
pink inside
reminds me of another place, my love.
Yes,
I take my time
and as I lay languorous over you,
I see my lioness self.
I see her feasting,
so thankful Oya has given a little of Herself this day
to feed my poor emptiness.
Red,
I see my lioness self,
muzzle dipped in red,
looking up lazily at whatever insignificance dares interrupt
this moment.
It is of no import
and nothing disturbs the golden feast.
I see my belly replete,
swollen with the fullness of you,
my poor ribs still sticking out
because I've been starving,

my love.
Yellow,
I think of you walking toward me
in yellow silk and golden sandals.
I think of silken tents,
red cushions, perfumed oils
in a place where
you come walking toward me, my darling
into my arms.
Red,
I think of berries crushed
under my tongue,
juicing down my chin and yours.
I think of your mouth a bowl of ripe ones
sugarsweet.
I feast and feast, greedy for you
and the bowl is never finished.
Red,
here we are
relinquished and surrendered.
Here we are, my love
yellow, golden under the sun which belongs to us.
Here we are
Black.

Every Touch

ANDREA FREEMAN

Not surprised by her message, I shock myself at the urgency with which I return her call, rushing to the phone and relieved beyond reason to recognize her voice at the other end.

Chatting nervously, I rhyme off names of famous women I lust after and encourage her to do the same. She catches me off guard, following "Nobody, really" with her confession: "I like you."

Wanting to respond immediately, tongue-tied, I can only sit silently, stunned and blushing in an empty room. "I can't believe it." I stutter, "I mean, I can't believe you feel the same way I do."

She seems so casual, so confident in her admission, I realize suddenly that I have undoubtedly, inexcusably misunderstood her. She likes me, what does that mean? She continues, telling me she feels it is women's duty to make each other feel good whenever they can. I reconsider her words in this less frightening but ultimately less thrilling light, relieved I had lacked the courage to react with a description of my own, recently discovered desires.

Disappointed but composed I turn the conversation to another topic, waiting until I get into bed to contemplate, marvel. Waves of joy jolt me awake when I begin to feel drowsy. For the first time I allow myself to think of her while I touch myself, my fantasy mingling with the sound of her voice, my closed eyes seeing her naked on top of me. I come quickly, groans echoing in my empty room, then finally drift into sleep.

After a casual invitation to her house the next day, I feign eager innocence when she asks me to stay, laughing when she offers to sleep in another room, if I would feel more comfortable. After sitting, stretching, lying through hours of television, precious lost time we admit to regretting later, we flirt awkwardly on the floor beside her bed.

With the covers pulled over our fully clothed bodies, she stares at the ceiling in the dark while I stare at her. Decisively, she turns on her side to face me, lifting her fingers to stroke my hair, asking "Am I making you nervous?" Every trip her fingertips make across my head brushes out more tension, transforming it into desire, anticipation, joy.

Our first kiss scares me. It is too uncomfortable, searching, unknowing; we must be incompatible.

Quickly I dismiss my fears as her fingers wander from my hair to my shoulders, stomach, nipples. "You have such nice breasts." The words startle me, her courage and ability to speak strike me as I struggle to concentrate, rejoicing in an unarticulated frenzy.

"You're so small. Your skin's so smooth." Instantly I want to repeat the words back to her, for they are so much more true of her; she is far more beautiful, soft, and enticing.

I run my fingers over her countless times, lost in the desperate conviction that I never want to leave this bed, this moment.

Kissing becomes electric perfection. Caught between its intensity and the incentive it offers to move on, I reluctantly relinquish her lips for greater intimacies.

She touches my shoulders, presses me down and lifts herself above me while I wonder at her boldness, wishing I had done her first, imagining myself pinning her down, sucking her nipples and lightly rubbing her clit.

Ten more seconds in her hands and I would have come, but I welcome the chance to indulge her, shake myself out of the overwhelming sensation of drowning. Bittersweet victory, she resists my control, teasing and making my precarious position more valuable in its brevity.

With my tongue, lips, teeth travelling across her body, I shudder at her pleasure. At the base of her stomach she denies me, crying out for me to stop.

This frustration provokes an endless array of erotic possibilities so that now, at home in bed and alone again, I play over and over the moment she sat, straddling my legs, rhythmically, methodically circling my cunt, so distant and connected, so naked and thoughtful. My muscles lift and strain to feel every touch ... every touch of her.

Coyote Learns a New Trick

BETH BRANT

Coyote thought of a good joke.

She laughed so hard, she almost wanted to keep it to herself. But what good is a joke if you can't trick creatures into believing one thing is true when Coyote knows truth is only what she makes it.

She laughed and snorted and got out her sewing machine and made herself a wonderful outfit. Brown tweed pants with a zipper in the front and very pegged bottoms. A white shirt with pointed collar and french cuffs. A tie from a scrap of brown and black striped silk she had found in her rummagings. She had some brown cowboy boots in her closet and spit on them, polishing them with her tail. She found some pretty stones that she fashioned into cuff links for her dress shirt.

She bound her breasts with an old diaper left over from her last litter, and placed over this a sleeveless undershirt that someone had thrown in the garbage dump. It had a few holes and smelled strong, but that went with the trick. She buttoned the white shirt over the holes and smell, and wound the tie around her neck, where she knotted it with flair.

She stuffed more diapers into her underpants so it looked like she had a swell inside. A big swell.

She was almost ready, but needed something to hide her brown hair. Then she remembered a fedora that had been abandoned by an old friend and set it at an angle over one brown eye.

She looked in the mirror and almost died laughing. She looked like a very dapper male of style.

Out of her bag of tricks, she pulled a long silver chain and looped it from her belt to her pocket, where it swayed so fine.

Stepping outside her lair, she told her pups she'd be back after she had performed this latest bit of magic. They waved her away with, "Oh Mom, what is it this time?"

Subduing her laughter, she walked slowly, wanting each creature to see her movements and behold the wondrous Coyote strutting along.

A hawk spied her, stopped in mid-circle, then flew down to get a good look. "My god, I've never seen anything like it!" And Hawk screamed and carried on, her wing beating her leg as she slapped it with each whoop of laughter. Then she flew back into the sky, in hot pursuit of a juicy rat she had seen earlier.

Coyote was undaunted. She knew she looked good, and besides, hawks have been known to have no sense of humour.

Dancing along, Coyote saw Turtle, as usual, caught between the road and the marsh. Stepping more quickly, Coyote approached Turtle and asked, in a sarcastic manner, if Turtle needed directions. Turtle fixed her with an astonished eye and hurriedly moved towards the weeds, grumbling about creatures who were too weird to *even* bother with.

Coyote's plan was not going so well.

Then she thought of Fox. That la-di-da female who was forever grooming her pelt and telling stories about how clever and sly she was. "She's the one!" said Coyote.

So she sauntered up to Fox's place, whistling and perfecting her new deep voice and showful walk. Knocking on Fox's door, she brushed lint and hairs from her shirt and crushed the hat more securely on her head. Fox opened the door and her eyes got very large with surprise and admiration.

"Can I help you?" she said, with a brush of her eyelashes.

Coyote said, "I seem to be lost. Can you tell a man like me where to find a dinner to refresh myself after my long walk?"

Fox said "Come on in. I was just this minute fixing a little supper and getting ready to have something cool to drink. Won't you join me? It wouldn't do for a stranger to pass through my place and not feel welcome."

Coyote was impressed. This was going better than she had planned. She stifled a laugh.

"Did you say something?" Fox seemed eager to know.

"I was just admiring your red fur. Mighty pretty."

"Oh, it's nothing. Inherited you know. But I really stand in admiration of your hat and silver chain. Where did you ever find such things?"

"Well, I'm a travelling man myself. Pick up things here and there. Travel mostly at night. You can find a lot of things at night. It sure smells good in here. You must be a fine cook."

Fox laughed. "I've been known to cook up a few things. Food is one of the more sensual pleasures in life, don't you think?" she said, pouring Coyote a glass of red wine. "But I can think of things that are equally as pleasurable, can't you?" And she winked her red eye. Coyote almost choked on her wine. She realized that she had to get this joke back into her own paws.

"Say, you're pretty female. Got a man around the house?" Fox laughed and laughed and laughed, her red fur shaking.

"No, there are no men around here. Just me and sometimes a few girlfriends that stay over." And Fox laughed and laughed and laughed, her long nose sniffing and snorting.

Coyote couldn't figure out why Fox laughed so much. Maybe she was nervous with such a fine-looking Coyote in her house. Why, I bet she's never seen the like of me! But it's time to get on with the trick.

Now, Coyote's trick was to make a fool out of Fox. To get her all worked up, thinking Coyote was a male, then reveal her true female Coyote self. It would make a good story. How Fox thought she was so sly and smart, but a Coyote got the best of her. Why, Coyote could tell this story for years to come!

One thing led to another, as they often do. They ate dinner, drank a little more red wine. Fox batted her eyelashes so much, Coyote thought they'd fall off! But Coyote was having a good time too. Now was the time.

"Hey Fox, you seem like a friendly type. How about a roll in the hay?"

"I thought you'd never ask," said Fox, laughing and laughing.

Lying on Fox's pallet, having her body next to hers, Coyote thought maybe she'd wait a bit before playing the trick. Besides, it was fun to be rolling around with a red-haired female. And man oh man, she could really kiss. That tongue of hers sure knows a trick or two. And boy oh boy, that sure feels good, her paw on my back, rubbing and petting. And wow, I never knew foxes could do such things, moving her legs like that, pulling me down on top of her like that. And she makes such pretty noises, moaning like that. And her paw feels real good, unzipping my pants. And oh oh, she's going to find out the trick, and then what'll I do?

"Coyote! Why don't you take that ridiculous stuffing out of your pants. And take off that undershirt, it smells to high heaven. And let me untie that binder so we can get down to *serious* business."

Coyote had not fooled Fox. But somehow, playing the trick didn't seem so important anyway.

So Coyote took off her clothes and laid on top of Fox, her leg moving between Fox's open limbs. She panted and moved and panted some more and told herself that foxes were clever after all. In fact, they were downright smart with all the stuff they knew.

Mmmmm yeah, this Fox is pretty clever with all the stuff she knows. This is the best trick I ever heard of. Why didn't I think of it?

Welcome Home

D. TARROW HARRINGTON

Remembering Celia...
The first. The girl-woman who gave me physical sensations
And emotional fulfillment compared to none then, and few since.
Remembering the tender shock as our arms drew each to the other,
And the far more powerful after-shock when our lips met.
Celia, youthful beauty, the delicately sculpted face feathered
By dark, short hair. Long dark eyelashes framing Caribbean sea-blue
Eyes. Soft, warm indentations between neck and collar bone asking
To be kissed. Giving way to the shadowy hints of the swell of
Breasts beneath the white shirt.
And she whispered, "I want you."

Remembering Celia...
Clothes off, standing in the flickering candlelight, giving sight to
Prominent pelvic bones narrowing to the delicate triangle between
Her legs. She, using the power of the scene to beckon me closer. With
Coy assertiveness she is lying back on the bed's downy comforter.
Enticing my hypnotic movement toward her. Me, tearing my clothes
Off, leaving a trail of random piles, evidencing the rush I was in to
Feel woman flesh to woman flesh.
And she whispered, "Come to me."

Remembering Celia...
Arms reaching upwards, pulling me down to her. Experiencing
Sensations through every cell of my being that I had never felt before.
Her hand taking my chin and drawing my lips to hers.
Two female beings form-fitted, breast to breast, mound to mound.
Contrast ... hardness of erect nipples, softness of woman-breasts
And she whispered, "Relax darling, be one with me."

Remembering Celia...
The total possession of will through that ancient rite of passion
As celebrated on the island of Lesbos.
She, taking the more experienced lead, rolling me over and placing
One leg between mine, touching the soft downiness of my triangle as
She eased my legs apart, sliding her hand over the womanly roundness,
Running her fingers around the lips of the opening and back over the
Small throbbing hardness. And finally inserting tender fingers deep
Inside the warm, welcoming wetness.
And she whispered, "Now, baby, now."

Remembering Celia...
Giving me that deep, primordial release, almost agonizing in its
Intensity. Then wanting to give back what I'd just received.
Rolling her on her back, seeing her face, running my finger over her
Prominent cheekbones. A sculptor appreciating a completed work.
Leaning down, tenderly plying her lips apart with my tongue. Probing
That moist softness within.
And she whispered, "Your turn to give."

Remembering Celia...
The second tidal wave of passion washing over us. Not the hectic
Joining just experienced, but its calmer counterpart.
That slow honey-like dance of passion causing rolling tremors
Touching as I'd been touched,
Holding as I'd been held,

Taking as I'd been taken,
And she whispered, "Welcome home."

Log House Building

KATHY RUFFLE

"D4!" rang out in the woods.

"G4?"

"No, D4!"

"Okay, D4!"

Someone on the truck stacked with logs scrambled around and hooked the tongs over D4. She yelled, and after the crane operator pressed a button, the log wobbled up and over to the house we were erecting. Fourth round. Only five more rounds and we could call it a day. But I had no time to luxuriate in daydreams; here comes the log and I gotta climb up to catch and steady it. That was my job, that and re-stapling any loose globs of insulation up into the V-grooves. Terry's job, the woman yelling instructions for which logs to put on the building next, Lego style, was to plan the order of the logs and get them set down okay. She was the brains of the job. I was the joe-girl.

I had volunteered for all this because it had sounded like fun, but I was starting to reconsider. The walls weren't going up as fast as I thought, the temperature was dropping, and the drizzle was turning into slushy white drops. On the fifth round I'd have to start climbing a ladder for every wall. Why didn't they build scaffolding! Why the fuck did the owner have to have all these corners and short walls? They quadrupled the climbing. Oh well. Part of the "fun" was watching Terry take charge of the operation, moving around to just the right place, anticipating what needed to be done, then doing it.

H4 was making its way over now, so I walked over to be Miss Hospitality and welcome it to its new home. Steady that swinging log, careful not to let it hit me on the head, reach down to grab my staple gun and give a few loose pieces a shot, then let Terry place it just so. Finished, I smiled at her and got a dark glower back. But I won out and got her to smile back. Yeah, she's feeling the strain too. It's going too slow, some of the crew aren't pulling their weight, "D" sounds like "G," and everybody's getting fucked up.

So I try to lighten her up: "Hey, did I ever tell you how sexy you are in those coveralls?"

"Yeah, right!"

"No, it's true," I protested, grinning. (And here she thought coveralls were just for work!) Little did she know I was being perfectly honest while she was being perfectly, well, delectable. Because she was big and strong, she felt oversized, but it was plain to me, watching her work, that she moved with grace and precision. Tiny ballet dancers don't have a monopoly on that skill. She shoved the log down a bit, then yelled "Down!" The chain went slack and she reached over to unhook the hooks and fling them away from the house. So effortless. I would have made it a struggle, a wrestling match with a silly, dangly pair of tongs. Big and clumsy? No, she was big and graceful, and I wanted to test out her grace later that night, in a warm, cozy place.

When the ninth and last round was done, it was pitch dark and I had lost only two fingers and a thumb to frostbite. Everyone in the crew had lost their tempers, but at least we knew the logs were tight and in the right order. Terry changed out of her wet coveralls (damn!) and we piled into her pickup. That is, after she put her clunky tools back in the toolbox and locked it up. From under the seat, part of her leather carpenter's apron peeked out, you know, the kind that has pouches for nails and a slot for the tape measure and a strap to hold the hammer. She had more stuff in her cab than the average household shed. I sat by the window, rubbing colour back into my fingers. Judy was in the middle, stepping on the carpenter's apron. Terry was disheveled, letting the truck warm up, and I was starting to hallucinate about hot baths and hammers with smooth, blonde oak handles. I made a plan.

We dropped Judy off at her house. She scurried up the walk to her girlfriend waiting inside, warm and cozy, no doubt with a meal ready. Why, oh why had I volunteered for this? Then I remembered my plan and decided maybe the goddess would get a kick from it too. After all, I made the goddess in my own image, didn't I? I said, "I have to go to your house to pick up my shoes, remember. How would you like it if I stopped in and rubbed your weary back?"

"Would I ever!" Her big hands stretched and gripped the steering wheel like the vise I knew she would have in her basement. She even drove gracefully.

We got to her house and she expertly backed her truck up by using her two side mirrors. I helped her lug her stuff in: her toolbox, her workboots, her chainsaw, her carpenter's apron. The coveralls, only recently filled out so nicely by Terry's body, hung limply over her arm.

"The house was a bigger chore than I thought it would be," I said.

"Yeah, well, they're not usually that complicated. Twelve walls and twelve corners are more than most people have. At least our job's over. I'm glad I don't have to do the roof job. If you thought the walls were hard!"

"You sure knew what you were doing out there."

"I should, by now. You didn't do so bad yourself. You're learning." How come that sounded like a backhanded compliment? Oh well, I was glad it was over. I put the shoes, the pair I had come here for, by the back door. All ready for a quick exit, in case the goddess frowned. I offered to take the first bath, so she could go straight from tub to rubdown.

My bath was quick, basic, and devoid of pleasant imagery. Wrapped in her terry robe, I puttered around her house, playing detective: what kind of person is this Terry? I made a list of twelve things about her judging from her possessions and their arrangement. The List of Kathy the Dyke. She did have a vise in her basement.

Her bath finished, we went into her dark bedroom where she lay face down on the bed, dressed discreetly in men's pyjamas. I straddled her thighs in a most proficient way. She told me where to rub, where not to rub, and how hard to rub. It had a familiarity to it. The flap was face down.

"Terry," I whispered.

"Mmmmm."

I had dismounted her and stood beside the bed. "Roll over," I whispered, in what I hoped was a tone halfway between pleading and demanding.

Some seconds passed. Her breathing had big spaces between them. She rolled over and the flap flared a bit. My big, borrowed terry robe was open to the belt. She looked over at me and I gently let my robe open. Underneath, the warm leather carpenter's apron hung from the hipbones, the way I'd seen them worn. The pouches hung down against me. Her strong arm reached out and touched my pouch. I was playing carpenter for the second time that day.

Ambivalence

JENNIFER CATCHPOLE

The woman I had loved is back; after months of separation, she's sitting on my couch in the afternoon sun, asking, with some dignity, if we could try again. I am cool, closed, polite. No, no I repeat like a mantra, hoping it will save me. I'm not feeling that old internal pulling at all. As we talk, my mind skips back over the months we spent together, the months apart; the torment of the former, the relative peace of the latter. Being single is simpler.

Our frequent arguments were trials of endurance for me. She'd cry, I'd explain, on and on into the night until I despaired of ever being able to get the kids up on time for school. It seemed she was always hurting. I'd finally retreat, alone and frustrated, to bed. But I'm also remembering our weekend getaways, flying down the long straight spit to the ferry in her shuddering car, throwing our bags on the floor of the cabin and ourselves at each other, fucking every which way for as long as we wanted. After, we'd nap awhile before cooking a relaxed meal together or taking off to gallery-hop around the island.

I couldn't have one without the other. I'd decided after our last breakup to shut the doors of my body to her for good. It was the only way. So I'm seeing her out, relieved that it's settled again. But she catches my eye in that fatal way, and all at once I feel that familiar rush and know: I have to have her.

With no explanation I grab her, enveloping her large body, hands roaming in her hair, pulling at her waist, kissing, ravenous. I lead her to the bedroom, yank her shirt up in one rough motion, her pants down in another. Tumble her onto the waterbed and climb on top. We roll. I feed on her, breasts and throat, ass and belly. I thought I'd taught myself that I didn't want her anymore. Right.

We slow for a moment, becoming reacquainted with each other's faces, but I have to have her, remember? How could I have forgotten? Mouths, hands, legs trying to melt together. Lush. Elemental. I find her buried cunt slick, opening hot — same as always. I'm not the only one who remembers. I ease in, nudging past familiar creases, knowing how she likes it, circling two fingers, my head beginning to spin, my body flushing, going into rut.

She starts to heave; she's a mountain alive, moaning, biting, squeezing random chunks of my flesh in her strong hands. Forgetting circles, I'm just fucking her now, in and pulling up, thrashing deep then push, push, hold it, as she comes and comes, yelling my doom in exquisite tones, my knuckles against her pubic bones, soaked. My hand is aching but I feel like God.

After, I hold her, stroking her tenderly and murmuring appropriate endearments. She delights in my new level of butch and she knows she's got me now. She makes love to me, fierce and cooing, and it's as if we've never been apart. She's biting my back, pulling up on the globes of my bum and burrowing down between them, teasing my breasts with her lips and teeth until I'm sparkling all over, fucking me with these short, deep strokes of hers. Oh I've missed her, missed this. Greedily sucking her in, my pores fill, her name leaps freely deep from my belly, and I'm coming, gushing, almost oblivious, but a thin slice of my brain holds back and observes: I'm in it again.

Lesbian Love Monologue

an excerpt from the one-act play
Hot 'n' Soft

MURIEL MIGUEL

*Lights full. Set is bare except for red glitzy backdrop. Muriel
enters and leans against backdrop with her hand
poised over her head.*

MURIEL

I was naked... She was naked. We were lying on a big round
bed, kissing and rubbing and nuzzling and sucking. She sucked my
toe. I painted Her toenails and blew on the polish. She had big feet.
Size 13... BIG FEET! She got up and went out of the room. How
graceful, and with such big feet!

God, was I excited.... God, was I clumsy.

I started to paint my toenails. I spilt the nail polish on Her fancy
sheets. I ran to the bathroom, got the nail polish remover. I cleaned
the sheets. Now the room smelt like remover. I opened the window....

God, was I cold.

I shrugged my naked body into my second-hand, grey Halston jacket. I curled up into the green velvet, overstuffed chair. I felt in my pocket for my gold cork- tipped, brown Shermans and lit it with my turquoise and silver covered BIC.

God, was I bored.... God was I excited.... I was both excited and bored.

She came in with two steaming mugs of coffee on a silver tray. She also had bread and butter and a white bowl with big, red, ripe strawberries. She put the tray on the bed. She bit into the strawberry. The juice made Her fingers red. She came to me and put a strawberry into my mouth and kissed me.

She puts her fingers into her mouth and licks them.

The goddamn telephone rang. She answered it eagerly, giggling into the mouthpiece.

God, was I excited.... God, was I angry.... I was both.

I kissed Her on the cheek, I kissed Her on the neck, I pinched Her ass. I slowly took my second-hand, grey Halston jacket off. She watched me. I laid down on the bed.

I watched Her. She hung up the phone, ran across the room and lept on top of me. She grabbed me by the wrists. She was trying to kiss me, I wouldn't let her kiss me. No! No! No!

Coyly turning her head from left to right several times.

She bit me on the neck. She laughed teasingly. I quickly rolled Her over, knocking the coffee off the bed and rolling Her into the bread and butter. I rubbed butter onto Her breasts.

She simulates grabbing Her by the wrists.

She tried to get up.... I pushed Her down.... She tried to get up.... I pushed Her down.... More butter.... She tried to get up....

I pushed Her down.... More butter.... She tried to get up.... I pushed Her down.... More butter. I slowly licked the butter off Her hard, brown nipples.

She bends over, leering at the audience, running her tongue across her lower lip.

The goddamn doorbell rang.

God, was I excited.... God, was I naked.

She gave me Her robe. It was a white heavy satin brocade with pink lapels. It fell in folds to the floor and swirled around my feet. I sat in the green velvet, overstuffed chair. I lit a gold cork-tipped, brown Sherman with my turquoise and silver covered BIC.

God, was I excited.... God was I jealous.

She points to stage left.

In came a very short woman with a brown derby. The short woman was very nervous.

God, was I excited.

I got up, took her into my arms.... I pulled back her head and kissed her.... I crushed her to my breast.... I pulled back her head, kissed her, crushed to my breast.... I pulled back her head, kissed her, crushed her to my breast.... I put my tongue deep into her mouth.... I picked her up.... I put her down and I said, "There!"

Looks stage right, indicating her.

This time she came in with pears and yogurt. The short woman would not sit down. I grabbed her and sat Her on my lap.

She simulates grabbing the short woman and putting her on her lap.

She was pouring yogurt into a bowl. She came to me and slowly squished the yogurt on my head.

Her hand goes on her head and pushed down over her forehead, she gasps.

God, was I excited.

If you want to know the rest, you'll have to do it for yourself at home.

THE END

Gloria and Me

ELLEN SYMONS

We were sitting on my sofa eating our usual Tuesday night pizza. Gloria was trying to convince me to accept her offer of dinner to celebrate the one year anniversary of my coming out.

"But it's a special occasion, Mo," Gloria insisted as I shook my head.

"It sounds extravagant Gloria, and you know I get embarrassed when people fuss over me."

"Mona, come on. It'll be fun for me too." She put her hand on my arm and looked me right in the eyes. This is what Gloria does when she really wants you to listen to her. We were best friends and all, but I was having a hard time accepting the notion of her paying for my meal. Even on a date, I like to pay my own share. But Gloria wanted to celebrate. After all, she'd supported me when I was coming out, holding my hand through the self-doubt and my break up with Garry. Maybe she really would get as much fun out of dinner as I would. "Okay, yes Gloria, I'd love to go," I told her.

"Great. Be ready Friday at ten-to-six. I'll pick you up."

Of course, on Friday Gloria was right on time, so I was scrambling into my socks and shoes as I let her in. She brought me flowers, told me I looked nice, and hugged me. I returned the compliment and hugged her back. We walked to her car, an old blue Toyota Tercel. It looked mighty shiny, as if it had just been washed. Gloria opened the back door for me and bowed. "The back seat, Gloria?" I asked, but she shut the door after me and went around to the other side. That's when I noticed Deb at the wheel.

Gloria got in beside me. "Hi Deb, it's great to see you," I said. "I didn't know it was going to be a party."

"It's not," she answered. "I'm just your friendly neighbour-hood driver, courtesy of the wine-and-dine package."

"Deb offered to drive," Gloria added, "so we wouldn't have to worry about a designated driver."

"Planning to get me drunk and take advantage of me?" I asked.

"Yes," she answered, and smiled back at me. That's not the kind of joke I usually make. I'm not sure why it came out, but it did, so I let it go and just settled back to adjust to the odd feeling of having a chauffeur.

"Next stop please, driver," said Gloria in a hoity-toity voice. Deb saluted and started the car.

We drove to Whistler's Mother, a favourite dyke hangout. It's not strictly a lesbian restaurant, but all the staff are women. You can come here on a date with a woman and no one hassles you if you hold hands at the table. Gloria ordered a bottle of my favourite red wine, Fontanafredda Barolo, to go with dinner, even though I protested that a whole bottle was too much and too expensive.

"Hey Gloria, don't go overboard. I don't want to use up your grocery money for the next two weeks. At least if you're going to order a whole bottle, let me contribute to the dinner."

"Mona, I certainly make enough money to be able to afford what I've planned," Gloria objected. "Remember that babe, what I've planned. So shut up and let me enjoy spoiling you."

As usual, Gloria ordered tofu in black bean sauce. I chose pepper steak. We dawdled over dinner, wine, conversation. We got cozy, all hunkered down in our chairs with wine breathing in our faces, the laughing, soft buzzing and clinking of people sharing food all around us. It felt good and intimate: sensual almost. I was thinking how nice it would be to go home and go to bed with Gloria.

Then I realized what I was contemplating and changed track p.d.q. It doesn't do to start thinking lustful thoughts about your best friend, even if she does have the roundest, most welcoming curves in town, a wicked laugh, and a glorious smile.

I was so relaxed that I'd practically melted into my chair when Gloria got up to go to the can. "I'm going to call Deb," she said, "'cause it's time for the next installment in this celebratory soirée."

"What's that?"

All she said was, "Pinch yourself babe, time to wake up."

"Gloria, you're cruel," I muttered as she strutted away, looking mighty pleased with herself.

Outside, Deb was leaning against the car. She opened the back door for me with a gallant sweep and bow. "Get ready for lights and action."

"I feel like a prisoner," I said, "being swept away to an unknown fate."

"Just think of it as a prolonged surprise party," Gloria told me.

"I'm not sure I like surprises," I groused. She called me a spoil sport, but we were both smiling. I was really enjoying this, although I was used to feeling more in control. It was kind of like having your wrists looped to the bedpost when your honey has her face between your thighs. You know you can unloop yourself and say stop whenever you want, but part of the fun is maintaining the illusion that you don't get to stop until she says so. 'Course you can't play that game with someone you don't trust. But I trusted Gloria and at that moment I wouldn't have run away if she had suggested finding a bedpost.

I did squirm a bit at that last thought. These fantasies definitely seemed out of place. Why ruin an excellent friendship? I've always been good (or so I've thought) at keeping friend-friends and lover-friends in separate categories. Of course I'd always thought if I were ever going to make plans to spend my life with someone, the most important thing would be for us to be best friends who turn each other on, rather than lovers who happen to like the same movies. The people you fall in love with are not necessarily the ones you get along with best over the long haul. Still, there was this Gloria-is-taboo voice in my mind that kept hissing, 'Don't make this messy, Mona. Give your head a shake girl, it's just the wine talking, and what you're thinking just ain't proper.' It sounded suspiciously like my mother's point of view which made me want to ignore it. Easier said than done.

Before I knew it we'd pulled up at the video arcade. "What are we doing here?" I asked suspiciously. I'm no good at video games, as Gloria knows by the superior attitude I always take when I refuse to play them.

"Mona, it's time for you to branch out a bit, stop living so safe, learn some new skills," Gloria said. "I'm challenging you to an evening of Space Invaders."

"Gloria, you're wacky," I said. My dignity was at stake and I could already feel it leaving me behind to fend for myself.

There was a fresh breeze in the air. Standing up and walking into the beeping, flashing arcade made me feel better. Deb's lover, Sangita, was there, playing some kind of King Kong game, and soon all four of us were pushing buttons and trying to out manoeuvre various projectiles. I wasn't thrilled with the idea of "us" versus "the aliens," but pretty soon I was figuring out which button to push to explode those little spaceships.

Gloria was on a roll. She's got agile fingers. Every time either of us racked up enough points to move to a new level, she'd slap my back or punch my arm. I was beginning to feel bruised by her enthusiasm. And the constant physical contact was not helping to distract me from my fantasies. After an hour or so we were all impressed by our talents in defending the universe and Sangita suggested we move on. "Where?" I asked.

"Did you forget the dance tonight?" Gloria said. "Not exactly in your honour, Mona, but the timing's good for a celebration."

"Next stop, the happy-anniversary-Mona dance," Sangita called, as she ran to her car in the parking lot.

Deb dropped us off at the door of the community centre. "Don't worry about saving us a place; we'll find you in a couple of hours to see what the scoop is about leaving," she said and drove off to park. Gloria took my hand as we walked up the sidewalk to the community centre. Now Gloria and I hug hello and goodbye and do all that casual-touching-in-conversation stuff, but I couldn't actually remember us ever holding hands before. I tried to act as though I didn't notice, but my hand was already sweaty. Buying a ticket offered me the perfect excuse to let go of her without appearing rude. I got out my wallet and started to take out twelve bucks for two tickets, but Gloria stopped me.

"I told you tonight was my treat, Mona." She handed two tickets over to the woman with the cash box.

"This was part of the plan?" I asked her.

"Yup," she said. "So get stamped and let's dance."

"Geez Gloria, you don't fool around when you decide to take a girl out on the town, do you?" I said. She pulled me towards the dimly lit dance room.

We stopped while Gloria bought drink tickets at the table in the hall. Then she grabbed my hand again and we moved into the big room, weaving through bodies in search of a table. In a dark corner at the end of a long table in the back of the room, we found two chairs side by side. "Perfect. What would you like to drink?" she asked.

"Soda water sounds good," I answered. When she got back we sat and sipped our drinks for a few minutes. I was beginning to re-experience that cozy, mellow feeling I'd had at the restaurant when Gloria stood up and said she felt like dancing. By this time the deejay was into the slow songs. I wasn't sure a slow dance with Gloria was a good idea, given that my thoughts had been fondling her all night, but she had my hand again and was moving towards the dance floor. It seemed rude not to follow.

We wedged ourselves among dancing couples and Gloria put her arms around my waist and pulled me close. I was sort of dreaming with the music, letting it carry me on a cushion of movement, my chin on Gloria's shoulder and my arms reciprocating her hold on my waist, when I felt a tickle on my neck. My brain said it was Gloria kissing me, but I didn't quite believe it. Trouble was my body believed it and nobody was listening to me saying it was imagination.

When her lips reached the hollow below my ear lobe I heard myself make a sound like a calf mooing, low and quiet. Jesus, Mona, take a breath, I thought. Count to ten before you stick your tongue in her ear. "Um, Gloria," I said, and she stopped kissing me to say "What?"

"Um well," I said, and she kissed me again. It was all I could do to breath and keep pretending I was dancing, so I gave up talking in favour of survival. Soon I knew I was gonna explode if I couldn't touch more of her body. I was more than a bit confused by this unexpected action on her part, especially as I had spent the evening battling self directed moralizing. I whipped through my mind for a get away line. "Um, I have to go to the can." I used the first one I came across. "Excuse me, sorry but — " I broke away and beat a retreat to the sanctuary of the toilet.

I sat on the toilet and breathed for a while. I got up and washed my hands for as long as I could. I dried them for a while. I pulled at my hair in the mirror. I pushed my eyebrows around and wished I wore make-up so I could have a reason for standing in there poking at my face. Finally, I decided to do my best impersonation of a mature adult, go back to the table and look Gloria in the eye. She was leaning back on the legs of her chair when I got there. I said "Hi" in the direction of my belly button and sat down.

"Hi," she answered. We sat there for a while without speaking.

Then I said "Gloria," at the same time she said "Mona," and we both laughed. "You first," she said.

"Okay ... want to dance?" which was not at all what I expected myself to say.

Gloria looked pretty surprised too. "I'd be delighted," she replied, took my hand, and we walked to the dance floor.

"Slow down, it's not a race," she said as we danced, tightening her hold on me. We started again, real slow this time, but I felt nervous. I seemed to be holding Gloria at a more than respectable distance from my hot and sweaty body. "Are you enjoying this, Mona?" she asked.

"Well, I am a bit uptight," I answered. "I think it's the crowd or something, I keep feeling as though everybody's watching us."

"But we know half the women here," she said.

"That's my point exactly, Gloria."

"Then why don't we go somewhere where we won't feel there are people staring at us?"

"Well sure, I guess we could do that, but where would we go?"

"We could go home," she suggested. "I mean, to your place — I mean I could take you home, is what I'm trying to say. Drop you off, that is. Do you want to leave Mona?" she finally burst out, sounding exasperated.

You betcha, snookums, I thought. "Okay," I said.

Just then Deb and Sangita came up and Deb tapped Gloria on the shoulder. "We're ready to go, gals, how about you two?" she asked.

"We were just talking about that," said Gloria. "I think we're ready."

"We are," I said, "'cause it's getting too hot and sticky in here and you could cut the smoke." The four of us grabbed our jackets and headed for the cars.

I closed my eyes as we left the parking lot. The night had been filled with unexpected events and I needed some time to sort them out. Within moments I felt Gloria's hand touching mine. I didn't respond, not at first anyway, because I didn't really know what to do. Or how I felt about it. All this hand holding and neck kissing were hard to fit in with my belief that Gloria and I were friend-friends. It was quite confusing, and I hoped if I ignored it, somehow

I wouldn't have to deal with it. But after a while Gloria began very delicately to stroke my fingers and my palm. Soon I couldn't help it, I felt my fingers moving in response. I turned to look at her. Her face was lit by the glow of the street lamps, and I could see she was looking back at me. Deb had turned the radio on very soft, and she seemed to be lost in the world of nighttime roadways. Gloria and I just kept holding hands and moving fingers. After that first exchange of glances I was too shy to look at her anymore, so I focused on our hands. I don't know where she was looking, but it felt as if it was at me.

We pulled up in front of my place. Deb parked and turned off the engine. She opened her door and got out, shutting it behind her, but Gloria kept holding my hand, like a signal to stay. "The last surprise of the evening," she said, "but it will only work if you invite me up for a bit."

"Well sure, if you want to, Gloria..." I trailed off into silence.

"If you're tired or you don't want to, it can wait — no problem," she said quickly. "We can do it some other time."

"No, I'm not tired, just overwhelmed — it was an action-packed night, and it hasn't all sunk in yet. You know I don't usually go to sleep before two. I'd love to have you come up; but you usually go to bed a lot earlier than this, and it's just, you've done so much for me already, I can't think what else you could still have to surprise me with."

"Well, I do have something and I'm not tired yet and I'd really like to come up."

"Okay," I agreed with some anticipation and we got out of the car.

Then I saw Sangita's car parked at the opposite curb. Sangita and Deb were leaning against it. "Hey driver, you forgot to leave the keys," Gloria called. Deb tossed them over. "Thanks." Gloria unlocked the trunk and pulled out one of those small fancy flowered paper bags with handles, the ones that cost a bundle and look real nice. I always want to buy one myself, but they just don't seem ecologically or economically sensible, so I secretly covet them. The bag had something heavy in it. We traded goodnight hugs with Sangita and Deb. Gloria took my hand and we walked up the path to my apartment.

Inside, Gloria moved toward the radio. "Okay if I put some music on?" she asked.

"That depends whether you're going to put on the shlocky stuff you usually listen to or something with a bit of originality to it," I teased.

"I'm in a shlocky mood," she said, and turned the dial to her favourite AM station. At that time of the morning, it was playing 'All Night Easy'; you know, the stuff without commercials you're supposed to get naked to.

"Would you like a drink?" asked Gloria.

"You offering?" I said.

"Yup, liqueur; how about a Grand Marnier?"

"I'd love a Grand Marnier, my favourite, but I ain't got a drop in the place."

Gloria was getting two glasses out of the cupboard. Then she reached into the flowery paper bag and pulled out a bottle of the orange elixir. Not the smallest bottle either. "Shit! This is more than I bargained for all round. You weren't fooling when you said you wanted to spoil me."

"No, I wasn't," said Gloria, "and I've really enjoyed pulling these tricks out of my hat all night."

"Well, keep pulling," I said. "I'm enjoying it too."

Gloria poured. We sat on the couch, talking through a glass and a half of the warm, sweet, delicious stuff. I was feeling gently tingly all over and incredibly well-disposed towards Gloria and everyone else on the planet, when she stood up and held out her hand to help me off the couch. "I feel like dancing, Mona. Will you humour me?" she asked.

"I'll do my best Gloria, but I can't guarantee I'll remain vertical for an entire song."

"I'll hold you up," she promised, and put her arms around me.

"Good thing you chose the shlocky station," I said, "otherwise we'd be break dancing on the furniture."

"I believe in planning ahead," Gloria answered.

We settled ourselves more comfortably against each other and swayed around a bit. My body was beginning to give me arousal signals again. I was doing my best to ignore them, but it was an unequal match. Then Gloria kissed me on the neck again. Game over. I melted against her body. "Gloria," I groaned, "if you do that again I can't guarantee that I'm not going to respond in a sexual manner."

"Good," she said softly.

I didn't really hear her. "I mean we're friends and I really care about you and I know you care about me but what if we ruin a good friendship, by making..." My words kind of sputtered out. Something registered. "What did you say?"

"I said good. Did you think it was a slip of the tongue when I kissed you at the dance?"

"I didn't really know what to think. Images of your naked body kind of got in the way of me getting a clear perspective on the situation, so I postponed the whole thing and hoped it would go away."

"Well, it's not going to," she said, and started to kiss me on the neck again. "So what are you going to do about it?"

While I was thinking, I curved my neck against her lips and offered her my ear lobe for attention. "I guess I'd better do something," I groaned as she bit my lobe and I felt her hot breath on my ear. I turned my face and kissed her, ran my hands up to her breasts, down to her ass, kissed along her chin to under her ear, down to her collar bone, over to her shoulder. I practically collapsed on the spot when she started to undo the buttons of my shirt. I thought my knees were gonna give out on me or that my whole body would pour into my cunt and I'd just swallow her whole.

I grabbed hold of her waist and pulled her down on top of me on the carpet. Gloria kissed her way towards my nipple as the sultry-voiced deejay told us she would be with us commercial free all night. I unbuttoned Gloria's jeans.

"Was this part of the plan?" I whispered.

"Well, let's say I was hoping it would turn out something like this."

"Why didn't you just tell me, Gloria?"

"Isn't this more romantic?" she asked. "Besides, I was shy. I wanted to get into it slowly, not just plump it out like a business proposal: by the way Mona, I happen to be in love with you and hot for your body, so would you consider going to bed with me? And I wasn't sure whether you felt the same for me."

"Yes, I do," I told her softly. I kissed her lips and slowly helped her out of her shirt. "Let me show you," I said, as I brushed her nipple with my palm and she wrapped her legs around me.

My Bodacious Eyes have been Making a Most Rude Intrusion

CLARISSA CHANDLER

I've been watching Rhonda
I've been watching Rhonda's eyes.

Big, smooth, shiny, and
Tender as a lakeside.
Carrying always that element of surprise.
Looking just beyond the laughter,
I become terrified and want to cry.

I've been watching Rhonda,
As if her secrets are my secrets,
But she has the dye
That will make me clean again
To laugh, sing, and cry.

I've been watching Rhonda
I've been watching Rhonda's eyes.

Her shy, flirtatious glances,
That subtle sexualness,
That keeps calling me out.

The way she allows
Sensuousness — to roll right out of her mouth.
Sassy but
Cool, Calm, Collected.

I turn my back, I hear this
Low, guttural laughter sing out.
I'm caught.

Orange, honey brown skin,
Elegant neck,
The slope of her breasts,
Those round, curvy hips.

Honey Suckle has just Got to be present.

I feel myself licking, biting,
Nuzzling in her cunt.
Running hands in spirals and circles
Along her thighs.
Allowing my mouth to explore the
Swell of her stomach that falls away into breasts.

I get the feeling I shouldn't be watching Rhonda.

Holding you in my arms,
Gliding my hands down your back,
Resting my hands at the hip and
Pulling tighter and tighter.

Placing kiss after kiss on
Eyes, cheeks, and rosy peach mouth.

Rubbing and touching,
Touching and biting,
Biting and licking,
Being inside,
Getting lost in the smoky, lush smell
Of women in heat.
The hard softness of skin on skin...

I've been watching Rhonda.
All of Rhonda and it's causing heat.

The Mammoth Powers
of Lydia Lucinska

ELAINE AUERBACH

A soft voice eased through the crackle of the intercom: "Yes?"
Something about the voice reminded Desi of the huge powder puff
her mother used to keep on her dressing table.

"Hi. It's Desi Bujak. I'm the one who called about the ad."

"Of course. Come in."

When Elana let her into her eighth-floor apartment, Desi
couldn't match the bashful woman who greeted her at the door with
the bold atmosphere of the apartment. She had expected pastel
pinks and yellows, but instead found an array of colours, high-
lighted by a predominance of red and orange.

"So what do you do, Desi?"

"I'm a student at the U. of A."

"What are you studying, Desi?"

"Cultural anthropology. What do you do?"

"I'm a dental hygienist."

"Oh, that's interesting," Desi said, fixing her gaze on Elana's
sensuous lips and long eyelashes. Desi had never seen such cap-
tivating eyes. They were luminous, probing. When Elana gave her
a tour of the apartment, Desi noticed how lithely Elana moved, how
intense she was in her descriptions of the co-op's rules.

"So what do you think?" Elana asked, smoothing her thick, red hair.

"Huh?"

"Well, is it big enough for us to share?"

"Sure, sure," Desi said. "The rooms are really spacious and the location's great. I can handle the co-op duties with no problem. But I think the most important thing is not whether I like this apartment but whether we like each other. After all, we're going to have to live together, right?"

A rush of pink came to Elana's cheeks. Desi hadn't meant anything personal with her comments. But those dark brown eyes of Elana's stared right through her, as if she knew how passionate Desi felt about women. Don't be ridiculous, Desi told herself. There was a crucifix hanging on the wall above Elana's bed and a photograph next to the TV of a guy with his arm around Elana. Elana was straight, no doubt about it.

Desi hastily pursued the negotiations, telling Elana she was quiet, didn't like loud music (a lie which she could correct by using her earphones all the time), never watched television, hardly ever had time to socialize, and kept regular hours.

"So what do you say? I *really* like the set-up and I think we'll get along fine. If not, you can throw me out anytime. A deal?"

Again there was a flush on Elana's face, followed by a nervous "Why not?"

"I'll move in this weekend, okay?"

"That would be fine," Elana answered, slowly rising and extending her hand for a shake. "You know, I've never shared with another woman before. I don't really need to, but I was getting a little tired of living on my own."

What other needs could she fill, Desi wondered, as she took Elana's hand and grasped tightly, reluctant to let go.

The man in the photo turned out to be Elana's uncle George, priest and protector. He had played a big part in making Elana feel so easily ashamed of her feelings. Elana's father had been killed in a construction accident in Vancouver when she was seven, and her mother had committed suicide in a mental hospital two years later. Uncle George had become Elana's very strict guardian. Desi saw Elana's excessive modesty as a thin camouflage concealing tremendous sexual power. Elana was beautiful, and because she felt guilty about what this would provoke in others, she was shy. Her shyness made her even more beautiful, especially to Desi.

Within a week of living together, Desi found she couldn't think of anything but Elana, wanting Elana to touch her. Elana didn't notice her restlessness.

Desi expressed her sexual excitement in mundane ways. Since she couldn't sleep, she dramatized her tossing and turning, sometimes pretending to moan while having a bad dream. Or she read into the early hours of the morning, wandering around the living room and kitchen, rattling dishes and papers while Elana slept undisturbed. Sometimes she hopped into a cold shower and then paraded her nude body in front of Elana, hoping her chilled, erect nipples would entice her. But Elana always blushed and averted her gaze, pretending to be picking lint from the sleeves of her sweater or listening intently to the news on the radio.

Desi made several attempts to talk directly with Elana about her desire, but each time she tried, an imploring look from Elana dissolved her rehearsed crystalline speech into a torrent of babbling nonsense. Her breasts ached and her crotch throbbed. Elana never seemed to notice Desi's discomfort.

Desi almost gave up hope. She felt lost, lounging around in a stupor in the Women's Centre at the university, flipping through journals and newspapers, when she saw the ad in "Snake Women of the World." On the back pages, next to ads for aromatherapy and rebirthing, she read:

"Lydia Lucinska — Lady of the Mammoths — Touch the Spirit — Talk with Lydia."

Why not?

But what kind of name was Lucinska? Polish? Desi's heart skipped a beat. If it were true, if this holy woman was from Poland, from that part of the world where her mother's side of the family had their roots, maybe she could really put Desi in touch with the power she needed to succeed in seducing Elana.

Lydia Lucinska was not an easy person to meet. First Desi had to write to a post office box in Jasper. She got back a long letter saying Lydia was fighting a legal battle with a printing company. She would contact Desi after the battle had ended.

Frustrated, Desi rocked herself to sleep in blissful self-pleasure, imagining Elana by her side. Whenever she looked at Elana, Desi's colouring would change to the same blushful hue as Elana's, a sign of the intense guilt she suffered for her obsession. She was just about to lose control completely and fling herself across Elana's bed, when a curt note arrived from Jasper:

Make no moves, silly poopchick. See me right away.
Lydia Lucinska (Lady of the Mammoths)

Joy filled Desi's heart. Lydia clearly knew how desperate she had become. Desi wasted no time travelling to a cabin in a clearing at the foot of Mt. Edith Cavell where Lydia Lucinska swirled her magic.

Lydia was an immense woman with long white hair streaked orange, purple, and red. She didn't have much of a nose or mouth, but she had a very loud, booming voice. Her breasts heaved and soared beneath her embroidered white blouse when she spoke. Lydia's appearance awakened in Desi images of her mother and aunts back in Niagara Falls. They shared some but not all of Lydia's features. A wave of comforting familiarity washed over her. Desi felt right at home.

Before Desi could speak to the holy woman, Lydia rolled off a litany of insults against the printing company and their accusations that she worshipped the devil.

After a long time, during which Lydia's venomous anger never wavered in its intensity, Desi lost all patience.

"Lydia. Excuse me. Don't you think you're too obsessed about this guy not wanting to print your charms? I mean, ever since I got here it's all you've talked about and quite frankly I didn't come all this way into the mountains to hear..."

Suddenly there was thunder in the room, a loud clamour that shook the log walls and plank floors of the cabin.

The thunder, Desi realized, was the voice of the Lady of the Mammoths, channelled through Lydia Lucinska.

"Well, Well, Well!" Lydia announced. "I thought you'd never get tired. Finally, you are ready for the ritual."

"Huh?"

"Poopchick, *you* are obsessed with loving someone who doesn't yet love you. I have made you feel what it is like to stand by and be a witness to another's obsession. What do you care about my problems with the printer, huh? But now you know a little about the inner feeling of the one who obsesses you. You have experienced the passage beneath, so we can go even deeper. To the next step, understand?"

Though she couldn't explain it, Desi did understand. She had an intuition that she was going to learn more about culture and anthropology from Lydia than she ever would at the U. of A.

"You told me in your letter that you are in love with this Elana Jupiter who is under the spell of her priest uncle, right?"

"Yes."

Lydia pressed into Desi's chest a black patent leather handbag and a Cover Girl compact.

"I can help you with your desire. But you must do exactly as I say. Otherwise, poopchick, no good. Understand me?"

Desi nodded and listened attentively to her guide.

When she returned home, Desi told Elana she had been visiting her sick aunt in Calgary. Pretending she was tired, she excused herself early and went to bed. When she was sure Elana had fallen asleep, she tiptoed into her room carrying the shiny purse and the compact. She opened the compact and placed the mirror under

Elana's nose to catch her breath. Quickly shutting the compact, she carefully lifted the bedspread. Beneath her waist, Elana wore nothing, which excited Desi, but didn't deter her from her deed. With a small pair of sewing scissors, she cut a few strands of Elana's pubic hair. Following Lydia's instructions, she put the compact and the hair into the bag.

It was weeks before she could return to Lydia. First, she had to wait for the new moon. Then she was delayed because of a paper she had to complete. Finally, Desi was back in Jasper with Lydia.

"So you did what I told you?" Lydia asked.

"Yes. Here's the purse."

Lydia held the purse against her breast and drew in a deep breath. In the middle of the cabin, there were many coloured strands of ribbon, such as are used in the costumes for Polish folk dancing, falling from the rafters of the open ceiling like a rainbow of cobwebs. Lydia attached one of the ribbons to Desi's chest. She began to chant and dance frenziedly about the room, weaving the ribbons in and around Desi's body. When she finished, she took a Mason jar filled with essential oils and spread them over Desi's body, creating a musky, vegetative scent that put Desi into a partial swoon. With caressing hands, she gently massaged Desi's breasts, nipples, thighs, and clitoris. Desi watched in awe while Lydia, with three quick strokes of her hands, moved Desi's hardened nipples and swollen clitoris into the bag with the mirror and the hair. Desi could hardly believe what she had seen. Before she could peek inside the bag, Lydia snapped it shut.

"Now keep this bag and jar with you at all times. When it is late at night, open the bag. Leave the compact inside. Pour some of the oil into the bag and shake it gently from side to side. You may do this only three times. The spirits of the earth will help you with their charms. Return to me when the moon is full. And here, take some of these strawberries. They make a good dessert."

On the trip home, Desi's main worry was what to tell Elana about the patent leather handbag and the jar full of oil she couldn't let out of her sight. She came up with a story about doing research for a class on the social icons of post-consumer society.

When she got home, Desi played hard-to-get. Even though Elana was wearing her tightest blue jeans and a white silk blouse provocatively exposing her freckled neck, Desi ignored her and devoted the evening to making a luscious strawberry shortcake. The berries were a treat that Elana hadn't indulged in since her mother had been locked up in a mental institution. While Desi prepared the cake, Elana told her everything she could remember of those precious times with her mother before her death. Touched though she was by Elana's yearning to share her inmost self, Desi pretended to be unaffected by her. It wasn't long before both women said a friendly goodnight and went to their respective rooms.

Later on, when all Desi could hear was the humming of the refrigerator motor, she placed the patent leather bag and jar of oil in the middle of her bed and began the ritual. She unscrewed the lid from the jar and opened the silver clasp of the purse. Carefully Desi poured a third of the oil into the purse, moving the bag from side to side to blend the oil with Elana's hair and the mirrored breath. No sooner had she done this than a cloud of purple, orange, and red rose from the bag. In the cloud of scented smoke, Desi saw the form of a faceless woman, a woman whose body had Desi's breasts and cunt. Aroused by passion, the magic woman ran to Elana's room. Desi could hear cries and moans coming from the room, moans she knew could only result from breast touching breast, from labia locked in a rhythm of passion. Shortly after, the sylph of the air returned to the purse. Desi shut it tightly before falling into a sound sleep.

The next morning, Desi saw the effects of the charm. Elana had been awake for hours, sitting hunched on the living room couch. On one side of her pale neck was a dark pink imprint — a love hickey, Desi thought — while her face was deeply flushed.

"Good morning Elana. Sleep well?"

Elana's eyes were a deeper brown than usual. She swept back her hair and sighed.

"No, I had a terrible sleep."

"Bad dreams?"

"I don't know. My body feels strange."

Desi wanted very badly to make love to Elana, but Lydia had instructed her to restrain herself as much as possible.

"Sorry Elana, but I have to get to the library to do some research. I may stay over at my friend Cheryl's tonight," Desi said.

Desi wasn't sure if Elana was disappointed at the news or simply exhausted from her intense night of lovemaking with the spectre.

"I'm visiting my uncle today," Elana said, "and I might stop by to see my doctor. I'm not feeling well. So I guess I won't see you until Sunday morning."

Desi thought she saw a hint of longing and regret in Elana's face. Nevertheless, she remained stalwart in her magic mission.

"Finish up the strawberry cake if you like. There's still plenty in the fridge," Desi said, bidding her goodbye.

When Desi returned later that night, Elana had already turned off the lights and gone to bed. Desi quietly entered her room, removed the purse and jar of oil from her backpack, and repeated the magic charm. Again, after she had shaken the handbag, up popped the magnificent spectre, her body glistening with pearls of moisture. In a flash, she leapt from the bag, dashed to the hall, and again set upon making love to Elana. Desi decided to follow her this time. Peering in at Elana's door through a veil of darkness, Desi heard the bed shaking. Elana was trembling, delirious, her red hair spread across the pillows in strands that moved in rhythm with her sobs of mounting pleasure. Elana sighed. Elana groaned. The hard nipples of the spectre rubbed against Elana's breast; the wet, downy tumescent vulva of the powerful spirit pressed against Elana's own swelling lips. Suddenly Elana rose up, as if awakening from a dream.

Desi scuttled back into her room before Elana could see her and feigned sleep. She heard Elana come in her room, stare up at the moon shining through the window, then leave with a sigh.

The following morning at breakfast, Elana was weary and redder than ever. This time, her entire neck seemed covered with the deep pink scars of intense love bites.

"I'm going to call in sick today," she announced.

It was only a matter of time, Desi could see, before Elana would be as deeply in love with her as she was with Elana.

"Aren't you interested in what's wrong with me?" Elana asked.

Desi felt her knees begin to shake. Her heart was practically wrapped around her tongue. She grasped hold of the kitchen counter until the moment passed.

"I'd like to talk about it," Desi replied, "but I'm going to be late for my class. Catch you later, okay?"

Elana did not seem pleased.

Again, Desi stayed out very late. When she came home, all the lights were out in the apartment.

This time, instead of opening the patent leather purse and mixing the oil, she decided to wait. Her instinct told her that Elana was not sleeping. Before long, Desi heard the floor creak and saw a shadow move across her bedroom wall. The moon was almost full, the charm nearing the culmination of its power.

Suddenly Elana sat on the edge of Desi's bed and began talking.

"Are you awake, Desi? I guess if you are you're probably wondering what I'm doing here. I don't know really. I couldn't sleep. I've been thinking about you. You've been such a good roommate and friend. That cake you made, it reminded me of my mother. I guess I'd forgotten a lot about her. George never reminded me of anything. Not his fault, really. He has more in common with men than women. I didn't know I was allergic to strawberries. God, I've had a couple of bad nights after eating that cake! The doctor says I'll be all right if I stay away from them. My neck looks as if I've been spending time with a vampire! But really, it's made me have all kinds of strange thoughts. Like why I can't be naked around you. What am I afraid of? You're not afraid, I know. All day long I stare at people from behind a mask. What kind of mask do I wear around you? I wish I knew what you saw. I wish you could help me destroy this mask."

Desi was astounded by this confession but stayed silent. She wanted so badly to reach out and embrace Elana, to draw her into her arms and cover her body with tender, feathery kisses. The magic of the moment disappeared in Desi's silence. She saw the shadow on the wall returning to Elana's room.

Desi wasted no time in returning to Lydia Lucinska. Early the next morning, she grabbed the patent leather bag and jar of oil and hopped a bus to the mountains. Lydia, of course, was expecting her.

"So, poopchick. How was the cake?"

"It worked wonderfully, but you fooled me. You drugged *me* with that oil and bag ritual."

Lydia laughed and laughed. "What you think, eh? Women make magic like those fathers at the altar? Cheap tricks, poopchick. We have a deeper spell to weave, you know. Older and much stronger. Takes time. Takes patience and love, real love. What comes from within. Every woman has this power."

Desi started to giggle, then laugh. An uncontrollable chuckling went from the soles of her feet to the top of her head. Lydia joined her and they laughed so hard that the walls shook and the wooden floors thumped like drums beneath their feet, a sign that the Lady of the Mammoths was very pleased.

"I thought those red spots were love bites!" Desi exclaimed when their laughter subsided.

"To those sick with love, illness appears as the unmistakeable evidence of intense passion," Lydia said.

"So I saw what I wanted to see. Whatever you put in that oil made me succumb to the power of suggestion! But tell me Lydia, if the magic was all *my* hallucination, am I hallucinating now? Does Elana care for me at all? Will she come to my room again?"

Lydia told Desi to go home and find out. To her great joy, Desi discovered that Elana was eager to share her bed that night. The love they made together was not an hallucination, not then nor for many nights thereafter.

Davina

CAROL CAMPER

It was eight o'clock in the fucking morning. I'm not a morning person. I hauled into work, nursing the usual aches and pains. I eased myself into shift change with a twelve ouncer of Ceylon Black and a dutchie. I was mighty glad the chairs were comfy. I prepared to slouch my way through the meeting but as soon as I walked in, I received a message from somewhere in the vicinity of my crotch: "Wake up, Carol. Davina's here!"

Davina, Davina! I'd first laid eyes on her two weeks before when I was on-coming and she was leaving her shift. My response was immediate. Visceral. I wanted to lay more than my eyes on Davina. There was something glowing, soft, and round about her that brought out the butch in me, just as some of the tough ones bring out my femme. Surely that hot, shy glance from her couldn't mean what I thought it meant. All I can say is that for the sake of professionalism, it was a good job we weren't alone with that huge boardroom table just begging to be occupied.

Well, here she was again and this time we had twelve hours to get to know each other. She was a real sweetheart, all right. She was loaded with charm and shooting me "I'm a naughty girl" smiles with just the right amount of coquette. I was a goner.

There's something special about an all-woman shift. The energy is intense and this one was no exception. What a combination of women! Chatty Lorraine, bright, nosey, determined to make you spill your guts about your steamiest secrets. Stoic, reedy Kate, tough as nails, celibate for ten years and ready to bust. And the delectable Davina. Blushing, bosomy, maddening, and married.

Naturally, the conversation got around to sex. I mean, who could help it with vibes careening around like ball-bearings in a round room. With my usual candidness, I relentlessly peeled away the layers of coyness silencing us, deftly aided by Lorraine, the expert. Between the two of us, we loosened tongues kept normally reticent by convention. Truths came gushing out. Confession is good for the sex.

It was clear I was not alone in my crush on Davina. Lorraine squirmed in her seat and sneaked not-so-secret glances at her. "She-who-is-not-shaken," Ms. Kate warmed visibly each time Davina giggled. How could she not melt? Like a lot of "straight" women, Davina thrived on this lesbian intensity, only barely realizing what was going on — I think. How she glistened! She was giddy. Her eyes shone. Was it the sugar rush from popping the sixth chocolate chip rice crispie square she'd made with her own sweet hands? Or was it the sexual melt-down that comes with the realization that three lesbians with forty years of sexual experience between them want to baptize you with fire?

What a work day! I settled into my subway seat, thinking of Davina, groggy from twelve hours of constant arousal. It was prime fantasy time. I went for it. I dreamed of Davina. Lovely Davina with breasts full and firm. Tantalizing as two dollops of whipped cream in a weight watcher's guilty reverie. I imagined those titues naked, nipples hard, ruby bullets strewn across plumped satin. I thought of her roundness under her gauzy ensemble. Yes, I was going northbound on the Yonge line and in my mind southbound on Davina's belly. I parted the front of her buttoned shirt to find her pantyless. I grabbed her ass and pulled her onto my thigh, where she slid into my hard grind. I licked her cheeks, eyes, ears, and throat. Her breath came short and shallow with anticipation. I murmured, "Breathe, baby." She sighed right away and I caught her lips with mine and pasted fat kisses right there and there and there...

I was squirming in the subway seat as we rolled into Finch Station. It was time to file away the fantasy in the lingerie drawer of my mind. Why? Because for the sake of my kids, I was on my way to "dinner in Dullsville" with my ex-in-laws.

But ... the fun's not over yet. Later tonight, when I get to my bed, it'll be Destination Paradise West for Davina and I, on the All-Girl Underground Fantasy Line.

Idyll: Four Days

CHRYSTOS

We laughed so hard when we arrived at the tackiest motel room in the universe, replete with formica/chrome table & two rickety chairs, fake wood paneling & a spectacular view of the parking lot. In the coffin-sized bathroom, only one person could barely turn around. If you used the toilet, your knees were in the shower. If you bent to brush your teeth, your butt was in it. The kitchenette was of similar magnificent design. I needed to lose at least 35 pounds to fit in the narrow slot between the stove & sink — so I usually cooked & she washed up. I restrained myself from taking the marvellous sign on the back of the door: *DO NOT cook crabs in this room as it takes days to get the smell out.*

However, as you'll see, the setting faded very quickly into the close-up of new lust/tentative love, where each curve is all that one sees & nothing is as good as the taste of her cunt rippling.

There was a colour TV, newer than anything else by 20 years, which we attempted to use as camouflage for our sounds. Not successfully, for the following afternoon, we got dirty looks from the crabby young husband next door. I was afraid we'd be thrown out because we're both so loud when we come. I'd forgotten that no one wants to admit publicly what great sex we can have — they can't complain without severely jeopardizing the myth that *We're only lesbians because we can't get a man.* Given how much everybody hates us — churches, governments, parents, schools, jobs, pizza takeouts, gas stations, banks — all the hate we have to shove off our backs everyday, we deserve hot sex. What a relief it is to be with a woman who is louder than I am, to never wonder did she come yet, or still, that awful quivering silence. I love to hear yes, uh huh, harder, deeper, slower & finally cries from the shaking belly I recognize as they rush through my blood on out the top of my head.

Our dear tacky motel was located on the Oregon coast near Oceanside, which is worth the seven hour drive from my place (also on a beach but one that is ringed like Malibu with houses, houses). You can walk for miles without hitting the barbed wire of Private Snobperty. The sand was full of amazing swirling patterns from the oil spills, which were quite beautiful, though I'd give them up for clean beaches. On the way down, broom blazed yellow beside the roads, with pale green rosebuds on the tips of all the evergreens. We drove under Blue Herons, Hawks, Eagles, an Osprey & some dark Geese very high up, going north.

We met three months ago at a planning meeting for a National Lesbian Conference where we spoke intensely about politics. I don't remember a word now, as we glide through each other going to marches, speaking out, seeing political theatre, which sounds like one of those earnest, sincere relationships with very little sex, but I've never had sex so good. Just good. Sex where you spend all day in bed & never want to go back to work or talk to anyone else or put your clothes on. Sex that breathes. Sex that makes us wet in memory at roadside diners. She blushes when I talk about her pussy but she likes it. I know perfectly well that *Pussy* is not feminist but *I love your vagina* just doesn't have the right ring. Pussy has sibilance like sex when you finally get enough or you could get enough if you didn't have to sleep after 25 years of trying. A few times getting enough but with other incompatibilities that soon soured into go away.

Have I finally figured out what I want with a woman & do I finally like myself enough to make sure I have it? We haven't fought since we met, we both consider this very odd, as veterans of long & short relationships in which we were always doing at least three things wrong & usually more; veterans of women who found our character flaws completely unacceptable but still wanted to go to bed with us, most likely so they could continue to tell us how angry they were about x or t. We joked throughout the trip about what we'd fight about without ever managing to get angry about anything. I'm accustomed to having a nasty battle about one week or two into my 4 or 5 or 8 year liaisons. It is important that we're both sober. She's accustomed to girlfriends who don't think she's emotional enough or she's too emotional or wants to spend too much time together or needs too much distance. I make her laugh, which is good, as she's very serious. She actually enjoys & appreciates me which is balm after years of fear, resentment, envy, anger. She is supposed to be looking for a job, I'm supposed to be writing a play and a novel. Instead we drove down to spend days in inner & outer seas. I brought sexy nightgowns I never unpacked. We were in bed so much I didn't have to bring any clothes at all. We planned every night to get dressed to go out for a fancy romantic dinner at the place just two doors away but we never made it. She bought dessert there one night & brought it back to our bed full of crumbs & wet spots. Once we limped in around noon for breakfast, neglecting to take showers, so that throughout the meal we chuckled as we lifted forks to mouths, smelling ourselves.

She is plump, round, with nipples who adore being sucked. She is dark-eyed with searing eyes in which I am calmed & held still. She is dark-haired with silver spider's silk weaving her years, dark hairs on her belly swirling down, her divine greed. I reel in her smell, wind, seaweed, her gentleness, her butchness, the way she leans over me, her arms are walls that shut out the noisy messy world & convince me that flesh sweet on flesh is all I care about.

Her voice is deep, dark as she says hard words, shivery words, cunt squeezing words, hungry words, tasting me, taste her.

Her mouth came looking for me nibbling my nape, her belly pressed into my ass as I turned the pancakes, smiling. The next batch burned. My hands on her ass playing with her crack as she grunts, my tongue looking around for that magenta spot who goes ahhh whhoooo uh huh.

Her thighs slapping my ears, I reach to catch her head falling off the edge. I'm wet to my knees taking her until I'm mindless need. She thinks she wants to stop. *No baby* I say *Give me a little more I can feel it in you* & she does, shouting over the feeble Motown tape.

I smell my hands now when she has just left breathing in the light I've touched   Pulling her back into me pushing into her my heart swirling   My eyes weaving our names   Her skin that rises to meet me instead of drawing away & the restless hours before I'll have her in my hands   again pulling off her shirt my teeth along her neck little bites   my tongue in her ear as she shudders half pulls away because it feels too good

& the restless hours before I have her in my arms again pulling hours & hours 21 long hours before my fingers are warm inside her where all the colours of life dance where she grips me so tightly my hands cramp I don't care & go on reaching into her pushing to our screams of joy wet glimmer of her lips tender rivulets roaring

In the evenings we went for walks when the tide was out, our eyes intently searching for agates, of which we found many.

for Ilene Samowitz

The Tale of
the Time Traveller

TAMAI KOBAYASHI

It was a story about the end of the world.

The traveller sat by the fire, her eyes flickering with the heat of the flame. It was a night of tales, stories told to pass the time, for there we were, stranded in the darkness, strangers all, waiting by the wreckage of the bus, waiting for the planes and helicopters to pull us out of this nightmare. For here we had fled, escaping the angry, desperate mobs, abandoning the palaces and plantations, fleeing the judgments of the day, fleeing history.

And so, I thought, this is Asia. The light was dying across the thousand-terraced rice fields. Even Jakarta seemed light-years away. As I looked down at the burning city, I thought, I should never have come back.

I, as translator, had sat by the radio, but as the darkness crept in, the bursts of static grew fewer and fewer. The tourists, stunned, for once without complaints about heat, food, or language, huddled around the fire against this endless night. And with this fire at the heart of the circle, drawing us together, against a silence unreal, this silence too still for words, the traveller spoke:

"I want to tell you a story, a story about my life. But the story has no beginning, so I will begin my story by telling you about all stories, about time, and memory, and desire."

(If the truth be told, it was precisely at this moment that I first took note of the traveller, as she folded her legs and faced our company to tell her tale. Yet in that gesture was the echo of another. But I had not yet understood, as you, reader, cannot understand. She alone of all the travellers, with the exception of myself, came from the islands. Yet it was difficult to tell which region she was from. I had mistaken her for a wandering holyman from the north. Yet, by the fire, I could not imagine how I had taken her for a man; she had such fine features, sharp and beautiful.)

The traveller gazed into the fire. As I studied her in this dancing light, I noticed her hands, small, drawn with the grace of a shadow play. The light, thrown golden by the flames, gave her face a beauty, gentle and ferocious. She looked up at me as if I had spoken, and she smiled.

"Do you know what memory is?" she asked.

I nodded. For this was the purpose of my return: to remember and to forget. But does a mother tongue ever release you, does a homeland ever forgive?

She began again:

"Do you know the story of Scheherazade, she of the thousand and one nights? Poor woman, she passed from the hands of a stern father to a man who slew his wives at dawn, lest they be unfaithful. Yet on that night, she began to weave her stories, weaving an unbroken thread that ran through time. Of treasures found, loves lost, the journeys and returns. She spoke her stories for life, her life. As a reminder of all that is lost. Scheherazade, her story entangled in her stories. She dies with them. For all stories end, do they not?"

In this silence the traveller's words floated over the fire, above the hissing wood and spitting flame.

"It is strange," she added thoughtfully. "The tyranny of the narrative, the seduction of the story, as if it could have been anything else. In fleeing a prophecy, one fulfils that very prophecy. Death meets the man in Samarkand. We fall for the story every time, falling, as always, to our deaths."

"Change the story," I said. "Change everything."

She smiled softly, softly. "Another story then. Simple enough. Once upon a time there was a time traveller. Now this traveller had leapt through many centuries, through so much war, so much pain, searching for a woman she could no longer remember. Searching for something once left behind that, if found, could end her travels, and perhaps even save the world. For you see, the fabric of time was slowly unravelling, thread by thread. The traveller, in attempting to mend the rent in the fabric of time, had became entangled in its net. One can only exist in a moment. And what is time but a moment, framed by other moments, a point defined by other points. Memory. History. But you see, as she slipped through time what she lost were those markers, wandering without past or future. Memory became prescience. And what was memory, after all, but a mere invocation of loss. Yet she could never stay with one thread, for you see, if you meet your double, you will die. One can only exist in one place at a time. If ever the traveller met herself in this search to end this search, time and space would collapse."

"How does the story end?"

"It never ends. The traveller dies in the past, to be born in the future, to die in the past..."

"Always?"

"Always."

And it was at that moment that the rains came.

"Come with me."

The traveller is shaking me from my sleep. I go with her, unthinkingly, up to the foot of the hills, slipping through the groves, until we find what could only have been a shrine to the god on the mountain. In its circle we build our fire, sheltered by the leaves that swayed overhead.

And there it is again. That gesture. A haunting, ghost mirage.

I shiver, whispering softly, "It feels like the end of the world."

The traveller's eyes scan the sky, the stars. She nods and says simply, "Soon enough."

I turn to her and think, she could be lying, she could be crazy. I see the furrowed brow, the strong line of her neck, her lips. She could be made of stone, this woman. Her eyes are hard but her skin glows golden in the firelight.

As if in comfort she says, "It's only a story."

This, I know, is a lie. Turning to her, I see the reason for my return. This is my riddle, and she, my sphinx.

"Who are you?" I am asking her. I can see the taut line of her chin, the softness of her breasts. "What do you want?" I want to ask her but the question dies in me.

She has stepped closer now. She is a mere hair's breadth away.

"There is a scar here," she touches my forearm, "and here," my shoulder.

"How, how do you know?" I stammer.

Her eyes flash and burn but her gaze falls. "I was there."

"The fire." That other fire that had burned in the city years ago. But I did not understand. "You can't..."

The traveller sighs. Her eyes are the softest brown.

"It is the time distortion. Abreaction. That horrible emptiness. I leave no trace. Except for you."

My voice is trembling. "You came back." It is not a question.

"Yes."

"Why?"

In this there is no hesitation. "Because I love you."

And I am leaning forward to kiss her, barely brushing her lips. Her hands stroke back my hair. She has spoken my name. She smells of woodsmoke and along her neck there is the taste of salt. My breasts fill her hands, my back arching into her embrace. I do not understand this thunder in my heart, this desperate longing. I do not understand. I am crying softly, softly, as the wind blows the rain through the leaves.

"For a long time I couldn't remember. It was that flash. It was a kind of blindness, psychic blindness," she said. We were lying on a bed of leaves by the crumbling altar.

"Was that the end of the world, that flash?"

"Yes."

"What was it," I asked, "a bomb, an explosion?"

The traveller shook her head. "No. A dream. You see, it all begins here. From what I understand, there are no bombs, no armies, but a simple dream in the mind of a child, a child dreaming about the end of the world. And in this dream, the child dies, and with her all that she had dreamt."

As I trembled, she held me gently.

"It is not so sad. We leave the earth to gentler creatures who know the measure of things, as we have never understood."

And yet, and yet.

"Will it always be this way?"

She leaned back, my head on her shoulder. "I don't know. It's in our dreams. As far as we can imagine."

"Or the kind of world we can't."

"Yes."

"Yes."

And she began her stories, her travels, across the sea to lands parched in dust, to mountains cut from heartstone. And to the north, the building of great walls and palaces, the rising of cities of silk, of gold, and older tales of the world's beginning. But speaking of the softer, smaller joys, the drums at harvest, moonlight slipping through the thatch, the eyes of a woman in dusk, she spoke of this and more, her story unfolding in a telling measured by the rustle of wind, a memory pursued by desire, knowing that this was spoken for me, for what I had lost in that fire long ago. I knew, even as the light flashes across the sky, that she would be coming back to me.

CONTRIBUTOR'S NOTES

Elaine Auerbach

Elaine Auerbach lives with Viviana in Waterloo, Ontario, at the foot of Lemming Hill. She teaches writing, works part-time as a free-lance editor, writer, and researcher, and volunteers as an assistant in horticultural therapy for seniors. Her short fiction has appeared in *The New Quarterly*, *Fireweed*, *Rites* and *The Malahat Review*. She has also published in lesbian anthologies including *Dykewords*, *Lesbian Bedtime Stories II*, and *Dykescapes*.

Karen Augustine

Karen Augustine was born in Toronto of Dominican parents. She has been involved in several group shows at A Space and the Ontario College of Art. Most recently, she has had work published in a lesbian of colour anthology, *Piece of My Heart*, put out by Sister Vision Press, as well as *Fireweed*, *Rites*, *Matriart* and *Diversity*. She is currently working on several visual/textual works exploring the effects of violence on Black women's mental health, and a journal for Black women artists.

Beth Brant

Beth Brant is a Bay of Quinte Mohawk from Theyindenaga reserve in Deseronto, Ontario. She is the editor of *A Gathering of Spirit*, the first collection of writing by First Nations women of North America and a catalyst in the development of the writing of Indigenous women. Beth has published two collections of her own short stories, *Mohawk Trail* (Firebrand, Women's Press) and *Food and Spirits* (Firebrand and Press Gang Publishers) and her writing has appeared in numerous feminist, lesbian and Native anthologies. She is a mother and grandmother and her laughter shakes the earth.

Carol Camper

Carol Camper is a Black lesbian mother seeking her true name. She is a writer, visual artist, performer and women's health worker.

Diane Carley

Diane Carley lives and writes in Vancouver, BC.

Jennifer Catchpole

Jennifer Catchpole is a 35 year old east Vancouver lesbian who mostly happily wrestles with single parenting, her disability (ME/CFIDS) and the delightful tribulations of dykedom. She has worked in several organizations concerning women's health issues and was a founding mum and editor of *Diversity: The Lesbian Rag*. She's written reviews but is currently trying to figure out how to write fiction. This is her first published story.

Clarissa Chandler

I am a writer, healer, facilitator, adventurer, single, and on the prowl. Life is great joy and anguish. I love living every experience to the fullest.

Chrystos

Born November 7, 1946, off-reservation in San Francisco of a Menominee father and a Lithunian/Alsace-Lorraine mother. Self-educated. Artist as well as writer. Author of *Dream On, Not Vanishing* and contributor to many anthologies including *This Bridge Called My Back*; *A Gathering of Spirit*; *Gay and Lesbian Poetry of Our Time*; *Intricate Passions*; *Making Face, Making Soul/Haciendo Caras*; *Dancing on the Rim of the World* and *Living the Spirit*. Indigenous Land and Treaty Rights Activist, working for the freedom of Leonard Peltier, the Dine Nation at Big Mountain, the Mohawk Nation at Kanehsatake and various other Native Rights causes. Proud lesbian for 25 years. Loving Tia to six nieces and nephews. Sober since October 1988. Make words, not war!

Lois Fine

I am 33 years old, about to become a proud co-mother for the second time. I am a Jewish lesbian activist with a penchant for pie charts and big-bellied women. Writing keeps my soul happy. This is the first poem I've had published in a book.

Andrea Freeman

Recently converted from intellectual to artist, Andrea's ambition is to spread a message of lesbian lust to readers and theatre goers everywhere. She also hopes to connect with other Jewish women and to survive without having to wake up too early in the morning, ever.

Susan J. Friedman

I am a 32 year old Jewish lesbian, born in Ohio and now living in Massachusetts. I am currently searching for ways to create a community that is both spiritually nurturing and politically challenging. I would love to slow down the pace of my life and spend more time on things (such as writing) that make me feel whole. I have been writing most of my life and have had work published in *Common Lives/Lesbian Lives*.

Addendum: I am also searching for the "real life" Ruth — has anyone seen her?

Carolyn Gammon

Carolyn Gammon is a writer and activist based in Montreal, currently living in Berlin. Her red hair and loose cunt are constantly getting her in trouble.

D. Tarrow Harrington

D. Tarrow Harrington is the author of a novel based on the persecution of lesbians in the U.S. military; a women's "herstory" book, which details ten years of the movement to aid victims of domestic violence and sexual assault, and three poetry anthologies. Eight of her poems have won national awards in the U.S. and twelve have been published in various literary magazines and university journals.

Tarrow, whose spiritual belief system is based on restoring and maintaining balance for Mother Earth and all her Beings, lives in New Mexico, U.S.A. with the beginnings of her long-dreamed-of lesbian/"fur-person" commune.

Jackie Haywood a.k.a. "Lovie Sizzle"

Coin Operator was originally written as a performance piece by Jackie Haywood for her character "Lovie Sizzle." Lovie has done stand-up comedy throughout western Canada and was a part of the 1991 Queer Culture Festival in Toronto. Jackie is a late-blooming lesbian in her 40s who is active in women and HIV/AIDS issues in Vancouver. She can be found behind the wheel of her '61 Ford Falcon or at home among vintage memorabilia, doing time at her writing desk, which affords a stunning view of the sunset on English Bay.

N. Holtz

N. Holtz lives in Montreal, is bisexual, a cook and literature student. She wears a lot of black clothing.

JAN

African-Jamaican, activist, lesbian, poet, Montrealer. Her fantasy fiction about corn and sex is tempered by the knowledge that many people on this earth go hungry or die of starvation every day.

K. Linda Kivi

I am a Kootenay country dyke of Estonian-Canadian heritage. "Report to the Community" is dedicated to all the adventurous mountain women whose antics are fodder for my imagination. I am currently working on my first novel and my book about Canadian women in music will be published in 1992.

Tamai Kobayashi

Tamai Kobayashi is a shy, reclusive Japanese Canadian lesbian plagued by telephone phobia and late night munchies. Her poetry has appeared in *Awakening Thunder: Asian Canadian Women*, Fireweed Issue 30, and *Piece of My Heart: Lesbian of Colour Anthology* (Sister Vision Press, 1991). "The Tale of the Time Traveller" is her first short story.

Muriel Miguel

A Native American from the Cuna/Rappahannock nations, Muriel Miguel's theatrical credits read like a history of alternative theatre in New York City. As the founder of Spiderwoman Theatre, North America's oldest ongoing women's theatre company, she has developed more than twenty shows and toured them throughout North America, Europe, Scandinavia and Australia. As a member of Joseph Chaiken's Open Theatre, she appeared in *The Serpent*, *Terminal*, *Ubu Cocu* and Megan Terry's *Viet Rock*. She is also a founding member of the Thunderbird American Indian Dancers and the Native American Theatre Ensemble. She has directed shows for Native Earth Performing Arts in Canada and originated the role of Philomena Moosetail in Tomson Highway's award-winning *The Rez Sisters*. Her one woman show, *Hot'n'Soft* is a howling celebration of lesbian sexuality based on fantasies, coyote stories, wet dreams, and personal experiences.

Kimberly-Lei Mistysyn

I am a Women's Studies graduate, presently employed at a gay and lesbian bookshop in Toronto. I have met the woman of my dreams and we are soon to be wed. Previous work has appeared in *Sorority*, *Phoenix Rising* and *Common Lives/Lesbian Lives*. This is my first major literary accomplishment. I dream of becoming a Vancouver resident.

Mona Oikawa

Mona Oikawa lives in Toronto. She is a Sansei (third generation Japanese Canadian). Her writing has been published in *Piece of My Heart* (Sister Vision Press, 1991), *Riding Desire* (Banned Books, 1991), *Diversity, The Poetry of Sex* (Banned Books, forthcoming), and *Our Lives in the Balance* (Kitchen Table Press, forthcoming). She is one of the editors of *Awakening Thunder*, issue 30 of *Fireweed*, the first anthology of creative work by Asian Canadian women. She is currently working with writer Tamai Kobayashi, on a collection of their poetry and prose, to be published by Sister Vision Press.

Kathy Ruffle

Kathy, forty-something, has published her coming out story in *Our Lives: Lesbian Personal Narratives*. By profession a librarian, unprofessionally she engages in cross-country skiing, softball, reading, hiking, cooking, badminton (at Gay Games III) and appreciating women's music, women's sports, women's films, women's drama, and women. And all that in a small city in B.C.

Ellen Symons

Ellen Symons lives in Ottawa, where she spends her time avoiding full-time work, writing poems and stories and being political. She is a co-editor of *Bywords*, an Ottawa poetry mag and sings with In Harmony, a chorus of lesbians and their friends. Her poems have appeared in a few little magazines. This is her first published story.

Karen X. Tulchinsky

Karen X. Tulchinsky is a Jewish lesbian, political activist, writer. She was born and raised in Toronto, and now lives in Vancouver with her lover Suzanne and their two cats. She is currently writing a lesbian/gay novel, excerpts of which are being published monthly in *Angles*, the magazine of Vancouver's lesbian and gay community.

Wanda Winfield

I am 36 years old and have lived most of my life in Toronto. I've been writing since I was 4 years old although this is my first published story.

I am a Christian, a lesbian, and a human being. That's how I want to be remembered.